Edward Laight Wells

Hampton and his Cavalry in '64

Edward Laight Wells

Hampton and his Cavalry in '64

ISBN/EAN: 9783337815578

Printed in Europe, USA, Canada, Australia, Japan

Cover: Foto ©Andreas Hilbeck / pixelio.de

More available books at **www.hansebooks.com**

Hampton and His Cavalry in '64.

BY

EDWARD L. WELLS,

CHARLESTON, S. C.

RICHMOND, VA.:
B. F JOHNSON PUBLISHING COMPANY,
1899.

COPYRIGHT, 1899,
BY
B. F. JOHNSON.

TO

CONFEDERATES,
LIVING AND DEAD,
AND TO
ALL OTHER TRUE SOLDIERS,
WHATEVER
THEIR FLAG OR FAITH, WHO WOULD
FIGHT TO THE DEATH IN A
RIGHTEOUS CAUSE,
THIS BOOK
IS
DEDICATED

PREFACE.

This book is intended to be a sketch of that portion of the military career of Lieutenant-General Wade Hampton embraced in the campaign of 1864, when he commanded the Cavalry, which was then an important part of the fighting power of the Army of Northern Virginia.

The facts related are based upon documents and letters in the possession of General Hampton and memoranda prepared by him, to which he has been kind enough to permit me to have access. Most of these were, by General Robert E. Lee's request, arranged for his use when he had the intention of writing the history of his campaigns. Other sources of information and verification, of which I have made use, are official reports and correspondence contained in the "Official Records of the Union and Confederate Armies," published by the United States War Department, and also authentic evidence furnished by eye-witnesses of the events, or by those conversant with the facts referred to.

It has been the writer's purpose to avoid in this narrative all exaggeration and artificial description, believing that the facts alone best tell the story of that momentous period, when the fate of the Northern as well as of the Southern Confederacy was daily trembling in the balance.

E. L. W

ILLUSTRATIONS.

General Wade Hampton .	FRONTISPIECE
The bather surprised by General Hampton	31
Colonel Wade Hampton, of the War of 1812, father of General Wade Hampton	53
Lieutenant-Colonel Frank Hampton, slain in the battle of Brandy Station, younger brother of General Hampton.	69
The battle of Brandy Station, Culpeper county, Va., June 9, 1863 .	89
Preparing for the field. From many of the humbler homes came many of the finest soldiers.	105
Map of Central Virginia	119
Wade Hampton, Lieutenant-General, C. S. A	143
An improvised hospital. This was a barn turned hurriedly into a receiving station for wounded men.	163
Capturing a Federal wagon train. Uncle Sam aiding the Confederate Quartermaster's Department	179
The explosion of the caisson, which seemed to give the signal for the victorious charge at Trevilian's, Louisa county, Va., June 12, 1864	207
Infantry capturing a Federal battery	221
General Hampton's sword	233
A night's rest. Typical scene in a Confederate cavalry camp.	251
General Wade Hampton of the wars of 1776 and 1812. The grandfather of General Hampton	261
Fitz Simons house, Hasel street, Charleston, S. C., birthplace of General Hampton	275
The beefsteak raid, Prince George county, Va.	297
South of the James	315
Lieutenant William Preston Hampton, A. D. C., mortally wounded at battle of Burgess Mill	331
Father and son	347
Lieutenant Wade Hampton, eldest son of General Hampton, wounded in the battle of Burgess Mill	371
A favorite tree of General Hampton's in the grounds at Millwood	395
Ruins of Millwood—General Hampton's home—near Columbia, S. C., destroyed by Sherman's armies.	417

CONTENTS.

CHAPTER.		PAGE.

I. BIRTH, ANCESTRY, AND EARLY LIFE—CHARACTERISTICS—SPORTSMAN—COTTON-PLANTER—THE WAR—IN THE INFANTRY—TRANSFERRED TO CAVALRY.   9

II. THE CAVALRY IN 1864—SUBSISTENCE, ARMAMENT, HORSES, &C.   78

III. POSITION OF THE ARMIES BEFORE THE OPENING OF THE CAMPAIGN OF 1864—SURPRISE OF KILPATRICK'S FORCE—DAHLGREN RAID.   107

IV REORGANIZATION OF HAMPTON'S DIVISION—COMMENCEMENT OF THE CAMPAIGN — WILDERNESS — SHERIDAN'S RICHMOND RAID—DEATH OF

CHAPTER		PAGE
	STUART—HAMPTON IN COMMAND—COMPOSITION AND NUMBERS OF THE CORPS—SHERIDAN'S CORPS, AND NUMBER OF MEN—HAWES' SHOP—MATADEQUIN CREEK—ASHLAND—COLD HARBOR.	124
V	THE TREVILIAN CAMPAIGN.	187
VI.	THE WILSON RAID.	229
VII.	PICKETING—SHERIDAN TRANSFERRED TO COMMAND IN THE SHENANDOAH VALLEY—DIVISION COMMANDERS ORDERED TO REPORT DIRECT TO HAMPTON—CHANGE OF STAFF.	250
VIII.	CHANGES IN THE FEDERAL AND CONFEDERATE CAVALRY FORCES, AND THE NUMBERS OF EACH—ENGAGEMENTS OF AUGUST 16TH AND 17TH ON THE NORTH SIDE OF THE JAMES—BUTLER'S SUCCESS ON AUGUST 23D AT REAMS STATION—BATTLE OF REAMS STATION ON AUGUST 25TH.	267
IX.	THE CATTLE-RAID—THE SCOUTS.	287

Chapter.		Page.
X.	Rosser and the "Laurel Brigade" Detached—The Fighting South of the James During the Last Days of September—Battle of Burgess Mill, October 27th—Five Forks and Lee's Letter to Hampton About the Result.	312
XI.	Camp Correspondence—Stony Creek—Miles Tries to Attack the Right Flank—Warren's Raid on the Weldon Railroad—End of the Campaign of '64—Hampton Ordered to South Carolina—Morale of Butler's Division—Capture of Kilpatrick's Camp—The Lone Damsel—Butler's Charge—"Buckland Races"—The Challenge.	368

HAMPTON AND HIS CAVALRY IN '64.

CHAPTER I.

BIRTH, ANCESTRY, AND EARLY LIFE—CHARACTERISTICS — SPORTSMAN — COTTON-PLANTER — THE WAR — IN THE INFANTRY — TRANSFERRED TO CAVALRY.

LIEUTENANT-GENERAL WADE HAMPTON, C. S. A., the subject of this sketch, was born in Charleston, S. C., on March 28, 1818. In Hasel street, within sound of the chimes of old Saint Michael's bells, he first saw the light. The watchman's voice from the tower giving assurance that "All's well!" had that day special meaning in the light of future events.

The great-grandfather of our General came from Virginia to the Colony of South Carolina previous to the Revolutionary War, and settled in Spartanburg District. Here he and most of his family were murdered by the Indians in 1775. Several of his sons, including the grandfather of the present General Hampton, were absent from home at the time, and thus escaped the massacre, and all of them afterwards served in the war waged for its independence by the colony against the British Crown. Wade Hampton, the grandfather of the subject of this sketch, belonged to the cavalry commanded by Colonel Washington, and was lieutenant-colonel at the battle of Eutaw. In all the fighting of those stirring days that cavalry was ever prominent, and the swish of Hampton's sabre always heard in the charge. This sword has been carefully preserved in the family of its bearer, and has the look of one made for use. The blade is much curved, broad, and scimiter-like, suitable, when wielded by a stalwart arm, for dealing telling blows, but not so well adapted for thrusting, which is now accounted more deadly.

The Colonial forces operating in this section at that period were small in proportion to those of their adversaries. They experienced trying times, but fought stoutly and well, and their work largely contributed to, if it was not decisive of, the final general result of the contest. Modern imperialists, who are carried away with the fallacy that God always favors the heaviest battalions, may sneer, if they can find it in their hearts to do so, at the smallness of the numbers of the Colonial fighters in this section, but one has never yet heard the Spartans of Thermopylæ twitted or belittled on the same ground. The authority of McCrady, the historian of

South Carolina, unsurpassed in research and conscientious statement, may well be quoted here:

"We shall attempt to show to how great an extent the ultimate result of the whole Revolutionary struggle in the country was dependent upon the operations of the partisan bands of South Carolina and her two neighboring States.

*   *   *   *   *   *   *   *

"We shall undertake to show that it was by these voluntary uprisings of the people of South Carolina, with the assistance of their friends in North Carolina and Georgia, that the whole of the enemy's plans were foiled, frustrated, and broken up, and the grand culmination of Yorktown rendered possible.

*   *   *   *   *   *   *   *

"We venture to believe that the record we shall present will show that no one of the thirteen original States of the Union suffered so severely in the War of the Revolution as the State of South Carolina; that in no one was there so much actual warfare; in no one was there such an uprising of the people; in no one was there so much accomplished for the general cause, and that with so little assistance."

The author from whom we have just quoted adds that he has a list of 130 battles, engagements, etc., which took place in South Carolina during the Revolutionary struggle, and that the records show "there was actual fighting in every county in the State, at present organized, but three, and that these three were traversed by both armies."

In the War of 1812 the Wade Hampton of Revolutionary fame was one of the generals sent to the Northern frontier, and there again he battled for the common cause of the States. That the military successes in that theatre were not more brilliant was due to no fault on his part, but to reasons not necessary here to revive.

The wars ended, the old General resumed his agricultural pursuits. He was among the very first, if not the first, to grasp the idea of the paramount importance, for his section, of cotton culture, and entered largely into it with the same good judgment and sturdy resolution that had distinguished his military career As a consequence, he amassed a fortune, and left to his descendants a very large estate, in which were comprised extensive tracts of productive land in Mississippi and Louisiana as well as in South Carolina. As we have said, he came to South Carolina from Virginia, the "Old Dominion," the mother, whose vigorous blood can be traced in a large proportion of the most prominent men of action in the South and West which our country has produced. Hampton is another instance of this descent. His characteristics were marked, and would have made themselves felt in any occupation he might have pursued. To his dying day he retained an imperious will, which would brook no interference with his own rights, nor tolerate it if attempted against weaker neighbors. To maintain right and fair play, and, in doing this, not to count closely the odds against him in war or peace, were his actuating principles, and those disposed to give heed to the laws of heredity, inexorable for weal or woe, are not surprised to recognize the same traits in his distinguished grandson. A little thing will sometimes better illustrate the bent of character than a greater. Old General Hampton in his later years was on his way one summer to the Virginia springs to drink the waters and take a rest. It was the custom of those hospitable days for the traveler to stop with his horses for the night and lodge at almost any convenient house where darkness overtook him. It was in this way, as local philologists assert, that was originated the name of a well-beloved Southern dish, "hopinjohn." At the door of a planter whose larder, strange to say, happened just then to be slenderly provided, appeared one evening the genial face of an acquaintance, who announced that he had ridden in to pass the night, and to him cordial welcome was given. Said the kindly planter, as he warmly shook his guest's hand, and conducted him to the house:

"Right glad to see you. Sorry I have nothing for you to eat except rice and peas and a chine of bacon, but we will do the best we can for you. Hop in, John!"

So John "hopped-in" doors, and for so doing deserves immortal fame, for he christened an excellent dish.

Old General Hampton, on the occasion above mentioned, stopped for the night at a friend's house, and, being an early riser, was found by his host next morning quietly sitting in the shade of a tree near the porch, on one of the branches of which were hanging the decapitated mortal remains of a huge turkey-gobbler. In reply to the look of surprise on his host's face, the old General remarked:

"I had to kill him. He was strutting about and beating all the smaller fowls, and I could not endure it. It was not fair play."

The unhappy owner of the offending bird admitted that his favorite's fate was deserved, comforting himself with the reflection how steadfastly the old gentleman had formerly followed the same principle in dealing with Tarleton's fierce troopers.

Colonel Wade Hampton, father of the present General, was a planter with extensive interests and large estate. He was very fond of thoroughbred horses, and raised some of the finest this country has produced. Noted as a patron of the turf, his motives were only the sport and improvement of the breed of horses, and not the greed of winning stakes. At his fine old place, Millwood, some five miles from Columbia, where the spacious mansion was burned by Sherman, was a private race-track, to be seen to-day, where his horses were exercised and trained. His heart was as large as his means, and his generosity as broad as his acres, and he was beloved by everyone. It was said he never was so happy as when presenting a well-bred horse or bull of pedigree to some friend, who especially admired the animal. His home was one where the charm of plantation life was well illustrated, and where fat, contented negroes gave living proof of happiness in their sheltered existence. In this circle, where kindly feelings and gentle, attractive manners held sway, unostentatious bountiful hospitality was to be found by all comers; planters, sportsmen, and men of culture, all worthy of it, found welcome without reference to the depth of their purses. Among others, George Bancroft was a visitor. That was in the days of the first editions of his history, before the results of the Civil War had induced him to re-write, in a different sense, for later editions those portions dealing with the States' Rights controversy. Times change and we change, it is true; but how can facts change?

A young friend of the Hampton family was, at one time, a student of the South Carolina College at Columbia, and each week, on Friday afternoon, was in the habit of riding out to Millwood, where he remained a guest until the following Monday morning. His horse he kept during the week at a public stable in the town. Now, Colonel Hampton was a trustee of the South Carolina College, and it was prohibited by the letter of the law of the Institution for any student to keep his horse, as it was supposed to be a source of distraction from studies. It was, however, a law more honored in the breach than the observance. But the Colonel was punctilious in his regard of rules, and could not countenance any infraction of them, and, on the other hand, was so kind-hearted that it made him miserable to interfere between his young friend and his horse. So he contrived a way out of the dilemma. One day he said

"I think you had better sell that horse."

This was, of course, accordingly done. When the following Friday came round the student went to a stable in the town to hire a horse to ride out to Millwood for his accustomed visit. But the stableman led forth a fine thoroughbred, saying

"Colonel Hampton sent this horse here and said he was to be kept for your use as long as you are at college."

Colonel Hampton was not much concerned in politics, but in war, true to his blood, he was to the front. He served on the staff of General Jackson at the battle of New Orleans, that brilliant victory won by the hardy men of the Southwest against great odds, largely composed of Wellington's Peninsula Veterans, the stoutest fight ever made on American soil, until the actions of the Civil War eclipsed it in glory.

He was sent as bearer of dispatches announcing the glad news of the victory at New Orleans, and his was the first authoritative information of that memorable event received by the President. Those were times before steam and electricity had been harnessed by man, and to accomplish his purpose the Colonel found it necessary to ride overland to Columbia, S. C., a distance of about seven hundred and fifty miles. Accompanied by his negro servant, mounted, and with one led horse, he performed the journey in ten days and a half, averaging seventy-two miles a day, including one day, when, owing to the streams being swollen by a freshet, only seven miles were made. In the greater portion of the route he traversed a very sparsely-settled region, much of which was wild, primeval forest. For three hundred miles it was necessary to carry subsistence for man and horse. Bridgeless rivers and swamps were encountered. He rode the same horse from start to finish, and, strange to say, the gallant animal was not one of his own thoroughbreds, but had been picked up by his father a year or two before from a cattle-drover, whom he had met one day on the road when traveling. The old General had the keenest of eyes for a fine horse, and fell in love with this one at first sight. So he stopped the man and offered to buy his mount. The fellow refused to sell, but was willing to exchange. "But, man," said the General, "my horse is worth five hundred dollars." "So is mine to me," replied the drover, and the bargain was made accordingly. No doubt the animal was well-bred, although of unknown pedigree, for he proved his blood.

At nearly the same time that Colonel Hampton made this famous ride, a very different kind of traveling party was wending its way from the North towards Washington. It consisted of five commissioners sent by Massachusetts and Connecticut, in pursuance of the report of the Hartford Convention of the New England States, to confer with the President of the United States in regard to certain amendments to the Constitution, styled by them "The Federal Compact," which they were to insist upon as a condition precedent to their States consenting to remain in the Union. When arrived at their destination these gentlemen found themselves in an awkward position and were greatly perplexed, for the first sounds which greeted their ears were the shouts of the people hailing with transports of joy the proclamation of peace. But, like sensible men, as they were, they concluded to make the best of the situation, said nothing about their mission, left the official documents in their trunks, put on evening dress and paid their respects to the charming hostess at Mrs. Madison's reception.

This was, in fact, a Peace Jubilee. In the rooms all was gaiety and happiness, every face beaming with smiles, but when the Commissioners entered a funereal silence fell upon the company. Matters were soon set right, however, by Mrs. Madison's admirable tact, and the pleasures of the evening resumed; but we may well doubt whether the five gentlemen in question enjoyed themselves overmuch.

In the sunshine of Millwood the present Wade Hampton learned the sturdy virtues "to ride, to shoot, and to speak the truth," and in its charming atmosphere was imbued with the refinements of life, acquired the scholastic knowledge suitable for a gentleman, and evolved the attractive personality which has exerted so powerful an influence on all with whom he has come in contact; which has made him dear to friends and proved a spell to open the hearts of his foes. This marked characteristic was of great service to the masses of his countrymen of the

North, as well as of inestimable benefit to those of the South during the terrible culmination of the Reconstruction Period in 1876. Then, in his State stood arrayed against each other—grasping their weapons—on one side education, intelligence, property, and civilization ; on the other, the reverse of all these—the negro and the carpet-bagger, leaning for support on the then existing Federal administration. The former demanded either a return of representative government, or else the rule of the naked bayonet pure and simple. This was no vague threat of non-combatant politicians or idle boys, but the stern—if despairing—resolve of veteran soldiers, well proven on many an historic field. If the fires of civil war had been then relighted no one can say where or when they would have been extinguished, but it is certain the effect on the North, as well as on the South, would have been lamentable, and not improbably subversive, eventually, of free government throughout the entire land. There was no man then living, except Hampton, able to stand forth from among his fellows as the Great Pacificator, who could extract out of chaos a *modus vivendi* between the discordant elements. This was rendered possible by his previous record, and largely by that indefinable personal influence which men, for lack of a better term, call "magnetism," and the conviction among all classes that he would act with generosity as well as with justice, and that the weak were as safe as the strong under the ægis of his protection. The inner history of this period, properly written, would prove very interesting, and it is to be hoped it will be taken up by some competent hand while there is yet time, for death is constantly at work removing the actors and those behind the scenes. Such an account of mere facts would indeed be stranger than fiction; would abound in pathos and romance, thrilling adventures, almost incredible situations, revealing much that is most exalted as well as most debased in human nature. It would exhibit a vivid picture of the most remarkable descent, for a time, to primitive conditions, which has probably ever been witnessed among Western nations since the days of 1793. Imagine the necessity imposed on every man, however averse to violence, of always—day and night, at his office or club, his home or at church—being armed to the teeth, ready at any moment to protect his own family or assist his neighbors, well aware that no remedy from law existed, but that a constant menace from its perverted forms was ever present.

The amiability of Hampton's nature was remarkable and it is not a little singular that, though personally the hardest of fighters, he was scarcely more popular with his own men than with those of his enemy Once in Virginia he came upon a Federal who was taking a bath in a stream of water, having left his clothes upon the bank. So the General quietly told him he was a prisoner. The man was dumfounded at this, not being aware the Confederates were near at hand, and supposing himself quite secure. He begged and plead to be let off, using every argument he could think of, perhaps (among others) that he was a non-combatant detailed to the Quartermaster Department, which at the time furnished about as many supplies to the Confederate as to the Federal army. The General thought it was needlessly hard to pick up the poor fellow in this way, but still he would have his joke. After amusing himself by letting his captive continue his supplications for some time, Hampton at length consented to let him go free, at which the man was delighted, and most profuse in thanks, and came ashore to put on his clothes. But the General said:

"Ah! No! I can't let you have them. My men are too much in need of clothes. I can't spare them."

After fruitless entreaties the Federal finally left for his camp, naked as when he was born, and the last words heard from him were thanks, and

"I'll name my first son Wade Hampton!"

Many years after this occurrence, the then Senator Hampton stepped into an elevator in a hotel in Washington; as he did so a young man said to him,

"Are you General Wade Hampton?"

On his replying that he was, the stranger asked if he remembered capturing and releasing a naked Federal prisoner at a certain time and place in Virginia.

"Yes. I recollect it perfectly," answered Hampton.

"Well," said the stranger, "he is my father. My name is Wade Hampton. Good morning, sir"—

and stepped out of the elevator at his floor

Early on the morning of March 11, 1865,

Johnston's army was crossing the Cape Fear river at Fayetteville, N. C. The infantry, artillery, and wagon-trains had nearly effected the crossing, which the cavalry were covering. Sherman's forces in overwhelming numbers were pressing up. General Hampton was near the hotel in the town, when one of his best scouts, Hugh Scott by name, galloped up, and told him that the enemy were close by in the next parallel street, a company of them having come through a by-road, which had not been picketed, and that more were behind them. The situation was critical. If the enemy succeeded in wedging in between the rear of the retreating army and its cavalry, the rear-guard, it would entail disaster The cavalry would thus be cut off from covering the retreat, and the bridge across the river, which it was essential to burn after the crossing was completed, if left intact, would afford the Federals the opportunity of swift pursuit. Not a moment was to

The bather surprised by General Hampton.

be lost. A cavalry leader must be able both to think and to act with the rapidity of a flash of lightning, and that Hampton did on this occasion. He realized that an ounce of prevention is worth a pound of cure in war as well as in disease, and that one man's services at the nick of time may be more valuable than those of a thousand a few minutes later. So calling to the scout and two members of his staff to follow him, and picking up three privates from Company K, 4th S. C. C. (Charleston Light Dragoons), then serving as escort to General Butler, and also one man said to be from Wheeler's command, whose name is unknown, and who was perhaps killed in the melee, the General dashed round the corner and gave the order, "Charge!" His seven followers (there were no others in the charge) obeyed with alacrity, and all, the General leading, flung themselves upon the Federals, who were drawn up in the street. These fired a volley with their carbines, but by that time the Confederates had struck them, and confused by the suddenness of the attack, the fierce yells, and the powder-smoke, they did not realize the small number of their assailants. So they tried to wheel about to run, but among them there were pistol bullets at close quarters, and the hack and thrust of sabres. Less than a hundred yards down the street was a turn at right angles to the left into the by-road by which they had entered the town, and by which they were endeavoring now to escape. Here they became jammed together in confusion, all organization lost, and their pursuers cut and thrust like devils incarnate as the fugitives probably thought. Eleven Federals were killed and twelve captured, and the rest, many of them wounded, fled in wild panic carrying consternation to their friends, with excited tales of hundreds of "men in buckram," as the best will do in such circumstances. Strange to say, so far as known, the only casualty in the attacking party was suffered by a handsome well-bred mare ridden by one of the privates mentioned. A rifle bullet struck her fair in the chest and came out just behind the saddle-girth, and yet the plucky little thing showed no signs of diminished vitality for ten minutes afterwards, and then patiently lay down to die. The pathetic expression in her soft, dark eyes would have elicited compassion from a heart of stone. Thus had Hampton grasped the situation, and applied the remedy, for the crossing of the river was then made without further trouble. The Captain, Duncan, of the Federal company, was among the prisoners. He reported his command as numbering sixty-eight by the morning report that day. There was also taken in the charge a Federal spy, David Day by name, dressed in Confederate uniform. When he was brought in General Hampton told him he had no time to attend to him then, but that when he had got across the river, he would have him hanged. The spy was turned over with the other prisoners to the keeping of some Junior Reserves, and when inquired for at night, it was found he had escaped from his guard. When General Hampton soon afterwards, in company with General Johnston, met some of the Federal officers prior to the capitulation, they told him that this man was one of the best scouts in the army, and that he had been captured three times since they had left Savannah. They also said, they thought, if he did not turn up the next morning after the Fayetteville fight, he would not be seen again, but that he reported on time. And now for the sequel and the point of the story.

Thirty-one years after this fight Hampton was in Denver, Colorado. A stranger called upon him at his hotel and spoke of having been among the Federals in the Fayetteville charge. Hampton told him of the spy in gray whom he had intended to hang.

"I'm the man," remarked the stranger.

"Well," replied Hampton, "I said I would have you hanged as soon as we got across the river. I certainly would have done it if you had not got away, but I am glad the hanging did not come off."

"So am I," said the other, laughing.

Day published an account of the fight in the local newspaper the next morning and was very laudatory of Hampton, and the number of killed he credited him with was fabulously large, when the correct bag was surely heavy enough to satisfy the most exacting. He was apparently quite proud of being connected with the General even in this way, just as others during the war took credit to themselves in being hacked by his sabre, if they lived to tell the tale.

Wade Hampton was a graduate of the South Carolina College, at Columbia, S. C., but received no military education. Many of his summers were passed among the mountains of

Western North Carolina. There are to be seen the loftiest peaks and highest plauteaus east of the Rocky Mountains, the scenery combining the grand and the picturesque in a manner altogether unique. As, standing on some height, you look northward towards Asheville, against the sky-line runs the long chain of the Balsams, crowned with the trees from which their name is derived, and further on the Blacks rise seven thousand feet in altitude, but wrapped to their summits in rich verdure, and of these Mount Mitchell is monarch by divine right. Nearer to you, but many a mile away, is Pisgah, of mountains made the queen by plebiscite, in virtue of her beauty, her profile clear-cut, like a handsome human face, with form soft, graceful, and lovely as some fair girl's. To the west are towering upward the Smokies on the Tennessee line, which countless ages ago in vain arose a mighty physical protest against the invasion of civilization. Close at hand are Whitesides and his lovable old comrades, hoary with age, mellowed, softened, and beautified by years, like those of our own kind with whom time has dealt gently. Southeastward, as far as the sea, three hundred miles away, stretches an immense plain dotted with towns and villages, farms and forest, but in every other direction are countless mountain ranges and their outlying foothills, in the distance not unlike Titanic waves of a vast ocean. Scanning the scene you soon detect the backbone of the system, the Blue Ridge, running north and south, farther than eye can follow, through Virginia and Pennsylvania, forming the water-shed between the Atlantic and Western States. Then you will probably be led to reflect upon the fact that this rocky wall and its gigantic flankers once represented the geographical line of demarkation, the racial "great divide," between the rivals during centuries, opposites in civil and religious creeds, the Saxon and Celt. You will recall that in the struggle between these for mastery in America, and in the world, Wolfe, dying victorious on the Heights of Abraham, pictures one grand achievement, but that the contest was finally and forever settled by Thomas Jefferson through the acquisition of that vast region, then mostly unexplored, known as Louisiana, extending, according to French titles transferred to us, from the Mississippi to the Pacific, and as far north as the Great Lakes.

Climate and scenery are moulders of body and mind. It is a belief, old as history and widespread as the family of man, that the mountain ranges and their rocky fastnesses have ever cradled the hardiest and freest of races. It is pleasant to think that this beautiful country may not have been without influence on the character of the greatest cavalry leader of our civil war.

By hereditary tendency and personal habit Hampton was an accomplished sportsman, and that region then abounded with deer and bear, as well as smaller game. At times, in the stillness of night, the fierce shriek of the panther might be heard. In the immediate section he frequented, east of the water-shed, near Cashier's Valley, there were at first no trout, although they existed at the time in the streams of the western slope. Hampton carried live fish in buckets across the ridge and liberated them in the eastern waters. They increased rapidly in their new habitat, and the finest of speckled beauties soon abounded there. It is said that he who causes one seed of grain to grow in ground which never before produced human food, has conferred a greater boon upon his fellow-men than anything statesman or warrior has ever accomplished. There must be credit due to him, then, who, besides stocking the waters with useful food, furnishes sport to the enthusiasts of the rod.

Hampton's skill as a fisherman was great; trout, black bass, and salmon could rarely resist the attractive cast of his fly, but no less attractive was his companionship to all sorts and conditions of men. Only last summer (1898) a friend of the writer made a fishing trip in New Brunswick, where he enjoyed fine sport. His guide, a past-master with rod as well as paddle, a half-breed, or rather mixture of many breeds, speaking English broken into small pieces and with much difficulty, somehow discovered that his charge was from South Carolina. So he said one day, eking out the conversation with gestures and many pauses:

"You iz fro' Sous Caliny?"

"Yes."

"Then the swarthy face lighted up and he continued:

"Me know one great, great fisher fro' Sous Caliny; kill de big salmon; much, much; tree, four year 'go. Right here!" patting the birch-bark canoe.

"What was his name?"

"He name? One big, large, grand Seigneur, grand Gin'ral—Gin'ral—Gin'ral"—pausing reflectively—"me no tink de name. Only one leg 'e iz."

"General Hampton?"

"Yiz, yiz! him, him!"

And the fellow beamed with delight and smiled all over.

But, fond of sport though Hampton was, many was the morning in Cashier's Valley when he neglected his rod, good-naturedly amusing children, teaching them to fish, sometimes with no better tackle than a bent pin, a piece of cord, and a light sapling, or "pole," as the "natives" term it.

Nor were the summers spent by the Hampton family in their mountain home a mere pastime of tourists, but of material and lasting benefit to their surroundings in the improvement of manners and morals. Many of the inhabitants of this sparsely-settled region were descendants of those who, coming from other communities, had left their country for their country's good to seek a refuge where trackless forests and mountains barred the service of legal process, and where the equally rugged borders of three other States near at hand offered a ready asylum to anyone too much "wanted" at home. It was related of one worthy residing in this district that his house consisted of only three rooms, but each of these was in a different State, and consequently it would require three sheriffs, from three different States, duly provided with warrants, and all present at the same time, to abridge this citizen of his personal liberty when within his castle. To these people in that day was thus afforded by the Hamptons the civilizing, educating influence exerted by those of gentle birth and culture. Fair hands and kindly hearts dispensed charity by gracious words and deeds in many a rude log-cabin clinging to the mountain-side, or nestled in the lonely "cove." No wonder that among them Hampton became a name to conjure by. Later on, towards the end of the Civil War, in that inaccessible section, military as well as civil power became practically nullified, and thousands of deserters from both the Federal and Confederate armies congregated there. Desertion, from whatever flag, "Nothing cans't thou to damnation add," not even slander of poor Desdemona, "greater than that," and well was this exemplified by this brotherhood of traitors, whose only article of belief was the socialistic creed that for anyone, except themselves, to hold property was a sin against "humanity." But even in those disjointed times all ears were not deaf to the spell of the Hampton name, and the traveler will still find it potent there after all these years.

Prior to the Civil War Hampton's very extensive planting interests were in Mississippi, where he usually resided during the winter months. The acreage which he had under cultivation in cotton the year before the war was estimated to be good for a crop of 5,000 bales, and, besides this, food supplies were raised. To give some idea of the value of such a cotton crop, one need but calculate what it would have sold for in New York at the average price for 1860 of bales of the weight then customary from that section, which would have been a quarter of a million of dollars in gold. At the average value of 1864 it would have brought three millions of dollars, or at the maximum price of that year four and a quarter millions in United States currency, but that was during the cotton famine and in depreciated greenbacks. The occupation for brain and body furnished by such a large agricultural business would be of an exacting character. The habit of command over so many hundred negroes, and numerous agents and overseers thus necessitated, was not a bad school for some of the practical details of war. But time was found for field-sports, and he was noted throughout that region as a bear-hunter, and was reputed to be the only man who, after killing one of these animals, could without help lift the carcass upon a horse to carry it home, a feat requiring great strength as well as skill.

In regard to Hampton's political attitude in the controversy between the Northern and Southern States of the Federal Union, little need here be said. He would naturally, we must suppose, hold the doctrines now styled "States' Rights;" for these were then almost universally current in the South and common in all other sections, having hardly been seriously called in question anywhere until the second quarter of the present century. He would be aware that these principles were not only orthodox, according to the Jeffersonian school, but were also strictly in accordance with the faith conscientiously held by a large majority of the best and most influential people in New England. Such well-known and esteemed men of that section as Johnson, Ellsworth, Sherman, Hillhouse, Quincy, Gardener, King, Lowell, Dwight, John Quincy Adams, and very many others had, as all well-informed persons know, put themselves on record as endorsing the most extreme views of "States' Rights," including secession, either by direct assertion or necessary implication. It was a matter of public notoriety that New England newspapers of standing and influence, as well as their public meetings and Legislatures, had declared absolute adherence to these dogmas, and the Hartford Convention had put for all time its most solemn seal of approval upon them. To anyone holding these views, the denial of the right of secession and oposition to it by armed force, would seem absolutely revolutionary, without any sanction in law—a rebellion ; and, like all rebellions, having no legal standing, unless acquiescence was obtained through successful exertion of physical power. To those of this generation, educated from childhood in the belief that the subject contended for in the war by the South was the perpetuation of negro slavery, and by the North its extinction, the inner history of the War of Secession will ever remain as a sealed book. Mr. Lincoln and the Congress of the States remaining united again and again declared, in the most solemn and candid manner, that negro slavery was not the *casus belli*, but that the preservation of the Union was; in other words, the denial of the right of secession was the cause. Undoubtedly the right to own slaves was an incident of the struggle, in the same sense as was the right to own houses, lands, mules, or any other species of property, recognized as such by law. If you desire to grasp the actuating idea which fired with valor the Confederate armies, you must first read their hearts and understand that they believed themselves dying, as their Anglo-Saxon forefathers were willing to die for "life, liberty, and property."

But to believe in the right of a State to secede from the Union was a very different thing from desiring the principle to be put in practice.

The idea that the writer has formed of General Hampton's views on this subject are that, like Robert E. Lee, he was very far indeed from being an "original Secessionist," but that he thought it his duty to abide by the decision arrived at by his State, and bear true allegiance to her. No one can for a moment suppose that men like Lee and Hampton, whose families had done so much towards winning the independence of the States forming the Union, would lightly wish to witness a disruption of the association. These were not penniless, embittered adventurers, but gentlemen of position, and when they pledged to the cause "our lives, our fortunes, and our sacred honor," they furnished three very substantial hostages for their good faith and the sincerity of their convictions. How many, on either side in the controversy, can say so much?

But the die being cast, there was no morbid, nervous hesitation on the part of Hampton. The season for argument was passed and the time for action come, and vain regrets worse than useless. He thought as the old Moorish king said when refusing payment of tribute to the Spaniards "Our mint coins nothing now but sabre-blades and lance-heads."

He raised the Hampton Legion, which he commanded with marked ability at the first battle of Manassas (Bull Run), where he received a wound in the head. This Legion was composed of six companies of infantry, four troops of cavalry, and one battery of artillery (Washington Artillery). Such an organization proved ill-adapted to the requirements of a great war, and consequently the different arms of the service were separated, and each became the progenitor of a famous body of its kind. It was *corps d'élite*. Of its original members two became Lieutenant-Generals, Hampton and Stephen D. Lee; one a Major-General, M. C. Butler; three Brigadier-Generals, Conner, Gary, and Logan. Many more were prominent in other ranks. Hart's battery, in which Halsey and Bamberg were lieutenants, and which thundered on nearly every battle-field in Virginia, formed at first a part of the Legion.

On the bloody field of Seven Pines, Hampton was again wounded, after performing gallant and effective service.

On July 28, 1862, he was transferred to the cavalry in Virginia, as Brigadier-General, his command consisting of the Hampton Legion of Cavalry (afterwards Second South Carolina Cavalry, Colonel M. C. Butler), Jeff. Davis Legion, Cobb Legion, First North Carolina Cavalry, and Tenth Virginia Cavalry. That brigade

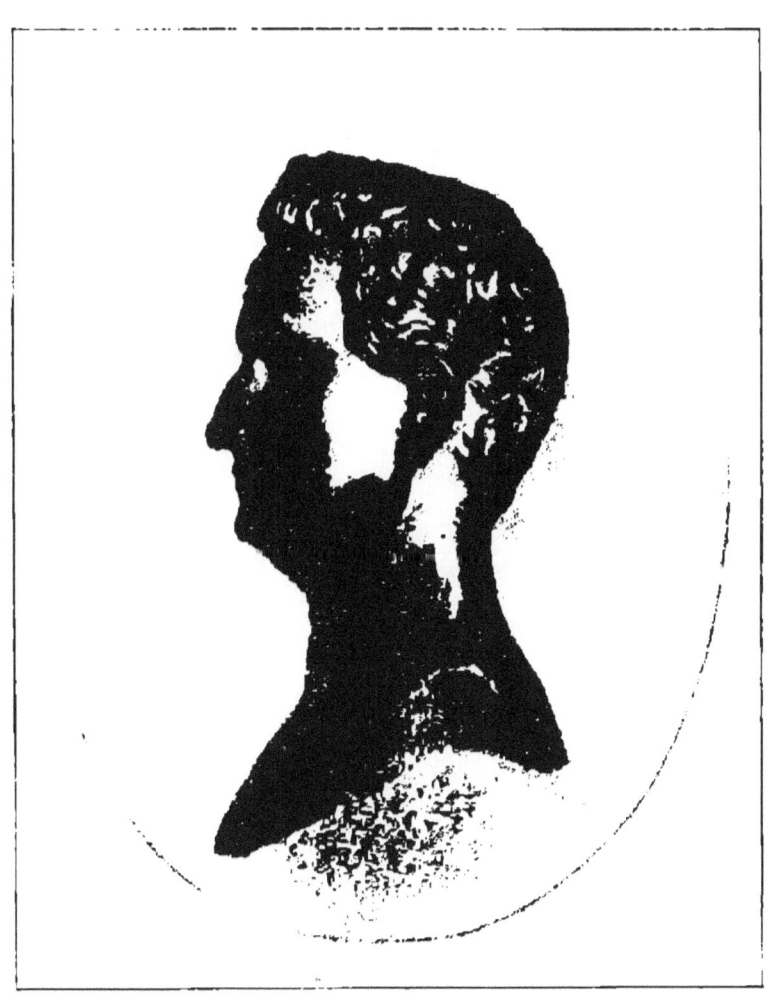

Colonel Wade Hampton, of the war of 1812, father of General Wade Hampton.
[From a bust by Powell, burnt at Millwood.]

figured very prominently in making the early history of the cavalry of the Army of Northern Virginia. At its head, and second in command of the cavalry of the army, rode Hampton in J. E. B. Stuart's famous raid in August, 1862, round Pope's flank and rear This Federal general it was, who issued some very spirited despatches dated "headquarters in the saddle." It was well, for he was left with little else. Not only were all the headquarter's papers, correspondence, and other property taken, but also Pope's private luggage. A full-dress uniform of his, all gorgeous with gold lace and epaulettes and profusely décoré with medals, was afterwards exhibited in the show-window of a store in Richmond and created much amusement. This was done in joke, by way of retaliation. It had happened that shortly before, Stuart, when accidentally separated from his command and accompanied by only two or three members of his staff, was very near being killed or captured by the Federals, and though he escaped, lost his hat and cloak. These were shown as trophies, and fun was made at his expense. But he vowed he would "get even," and this he accomplished in a more than ample manner, as just described.

In the Chambersburg raid in Pennsylvania (October, 1862,) Hampton was at the front as second in command. It was an expedition memorable for its daring and success, but, better still, for the magnificent discipline of the troops, and the scrupulous respect for private property which always characterized their movements. Only subsistence was taken, and horses impressed, and for these regular official receipts were in all cases given according to the system practiced by civilized armies, thus furnishing a voucher entitling the owner to make claim to compensation by his own government. The nature of their conduct was brought into unusual prominence through the accounts of the affair written by Colonel A. K. McClure, of the

Philadelphia *Times*. This gentleman had a "model farm" at the outskirts of Chambersburg, and was one of three citizens who surrendered the place to General Hampton, to whom Stuart had assigned the duty of preserving good order. He thus describes his first meeting with General Hampton when acting as one of the town committee:

"After traveling a mile westward we were brought to a halt by a squad of mounted men, and were informed that General Hampton was one of the party to whom we should address ourselves. It was so dark that I could not distinguish him from any of his men. Upon being informed that we were a committee of citizens, and that there was no organized force in the town, and no military commander at the post, he stated, in a respectful and soldier-like manner, that he commanded the advance of the Confederate troops, that he knew resistance would be vain, and he wished the citizens to be fully advised of his purpose so as to avoid needless loss of life and wanton destruction of property. He said that he had been fired upon at Mercersburg and Campbellstown and had great difficulty in restraining his troops. He assured us that he would scrupulously protect the citizens, would allow no soldiers to enter public or private houses, unless under command of an officer upon legitimate business; that he would take such private property as he needed for his government or troops, but that he would do so under officers who would allow no wanton destruction, and would give receipt for the same, if desired, so that claim might be made therefor against the United States Government. All property belonging to or used by the United States he stated he would use or destroy at his pleasure, and the wounded in hospitals would be paroled. Being a United States officer myself I naturally felt some anxiety to know what my fate might be, if he should discover me, and I modestly suggested that there might be some United States officers in the town in charge of the wounded, stores, or of recruiting offices, and asked what disposition he would make of them. He answered that he would parole them, unless he should have special reasons for not doing so; and he warned us that none such should be instructed by us to leave the town.

* * * * * * * *

"I resolved to stay, as I felt so bound by the terms of surrender, and take my chances of discovery and parole."

One can hardly avoid laughing now on reading McClure's story—so quiet, agreeable, and gentlemanly did he find these fierce-reputed sabreurs, whose names then were in all men's mouths. While occupying the town some of the officers accepted his invitation to take coffee and smoke with him in his library, and they had a pleasant time together Not only this, but he relates that not a private ever drew water from the well without first asking his permission and afterwards "giving a profusion of thanks." He could not help liking them and admiring, too, their fine soldierly appearance; but all the while there was an uneasy feeling lest these pet lions devour him all of a sudden, especially as he was at the time a United States officer. Like a hen with a brood of ducks he was in constant dread of some awkward thing happening. But when at length the bugle sounded and they took their leave, and not one of those Alderney calves on the model farm, of which he was so proud, had been disturbed; nor even a single one of those fine, big trout in the cool spring he loved so well; nor the beautiful, tempting pears, all ripe and luscious, he breathed freer, and was thankful to speed the parting guests, of whom, however agreeable, he stood in some awe.

It was upon this raid that the baby-eating joke was made, which went the rounds at the time. A trooper, grim and sunburnt in face, with dust-stained, weather-worn clothes and empty stomach, stopped at a house and asked for a morsel of food, for which he was ready to pay. The men of the family had fled, but there were several women at home, who peered with curiosity and alarm at the unwelcome visitor, and one of them had with her a baby. When asked for food they refused to give it, protesting they had none.

"Well," said the half-starved cavalryman, affecting a fierce expression and eyeing the baby with an ogreish look, "I believe I am hungry enough to eat a nice, fat baby."

Exit instanter the mother in horror, pressing the infant to her bosom, and quickly a plentiful meal was tendered to the child-eater to dampen temporarily the appetite for his normal diet.

The Chambersburg raid was made under

Stuart's orders, but Hampton was second in command, and upon him, therefore, would have fallen the responsibility of bringing the cavalry out safely, if an unfortunate chance bullet had ended the chief's career The seal of success, with most of us, suffices in military matters—the end gained justifies in this sense the means, but still there were such great risks necessarily to be encountered upon this expedition, so much depended upon good luck as well as good management, and the loss of the cavalry by capture or destruction would have been a disaster so grievous, that it may, perhaps, be questioned whether the proportion between the *quid* and the *quo* was favorable ; the Frenchman might possibly have remarked about it, as he did of the Balaklava charge, that it was "magnificent, but not war." The fruits of success were not offset by any disasters, but in themselves were not great.

On October 9th this raid was begun, the

force being one thousand eight hundred picked men, taken in equal numbers from the brigades of Hampton, Fitz Lee, and Robertson. The destination and purpose were kept secret from all, but an inspiring address was issued to the troops. Starting from Darksville, some fifteen miles north of Winchester, a northerly course was taken, and Hedgesville reached after dark, where the command quietly bivouacked that night, so as to escape observation by the Federal signal station on the opposite side of the Potomac. From here during the night General Hampton personally reconnoitred the ford at McCoys, about five miles distant, and selected the place for crossing. Thirty men were detailed to rush across the river at daylight and demolish the picket stationed there, which they succeeded in doing, cutting them off from their reserve and thus preventing a report of the attack being made. M. C. Butler, who was in command of Hampton's advance, was on the *qui vive*, and as soon as he heard the sounds indicating that the attack on the picket was being made, galloped into the river and quickly possessed himself of the ford. The advance was immediately resumed in nearly the same direction as on the previous day, and the Hagerstown turnpike was crossed at right angles. Near here was a Federal signal station, which was captured, and news of the raid thus prevented from being immediately forwarded. A division of infantry had passed along this road that morning, and Butler, favored by the screen of fog, rode so close to their rear as to pick up ten prisoners who were straggling somewhat behind the main column. Information, however, of the raid was imparted to the Federals by country people, but the news could not be promptly communicated where most wanted, because of the remoteness of the route from telegraph lines and railroads. General McClellan was at the time suspicious of an intended expedition by the cavalry, and was on the watch, but was looking for them in the wrong places. The farmers in Pennsylvania were so astounded at the appearance of the Confederate cavalry among them that many mistook them for Federals, and were left under that impression. Chambersburg was reached about eight o'clock at night on October 10th. The next morning ordnance and other Government stores were destroyed and the return march began. Unfortunately rain had set in, which caused anxiety lest the crossing of the Potomac should be obstructed by high water, and so it was a race which should reach the ford first, the cavalry or the swollen mountain streams. M. C. Butler, who, in the forward movement, had led the advance, now conducted the rear guard. Stuart was well aware that by this time the Federals in every direction were aroused, and that it would furnish him a difficult task to elude the numerous bodies sent out in pursuit of him, and to cut through their lines at a point enabling him to cross the river back to "Old Virginia." He concluded they would expect him to retreat by the shortest route westerly, and would be looking most actively for him there ; so he adopted the oppoite course. Taking the road east, in the direction of Gettysburg, he turned off at right angles at Cashtown and pursued thence a southerly route. The cavalry crossed the Maryland line, and when Emmitsburg was reached were the recipients of an enthusiastic welcome from the inhabitants. Meantime the Federal infantry as well as cavalry were scurrying about seeking the raiders, disproving the saying, "Seek, and ye shall find." At Mechanicstown, Pleasanton, with his command of Federal cavalry, was within four miles of them, but was not aware of it at the time. At Emmitsburg, where the Confederates had arrived about dark, some troopers belonging to a detachment of Pennsylvania cavalry were captured. From there the Potomac was distant forty-five miles southerly, and for it on a trot through the night rode the raiders. Dodging by turns and skirmishing with bodies of Federals, they reached the river at White's Ford about eight o'clock in the morning. The crossing was held by hostile infantry, but a bold demonstration caused them to retreat. From all sides, however, their foes were pouring forward to cut them off. But across the river, in spite of them, rode the cavalry—all but Butler and his rear guard, who were skirmishing to cover the ford. Four couriers had been sent to order him to come back with all possible haste; the enemy were closing in with large numbers— his escape seemed impossible. Another messenger—an officer—was despatched to him as a last chance, to order him to withdraw at a gallop. But Butler replied that he feared he could not save his gun.

"Leave your gun, then, and come."

"I don't want to lose it," answered Butler with his invariable *sang-froid*, "but we will see what we can do."

And to the great surprise of all, he brought off his gun and every man, and as they came galloping round the turn of the road and into the ford amidst the scattering bullets of the enemy, the delight of the beholders broke out into a cheer And thus the raid came to a triumphant end. The march from Chambersburg was eighty miles in length, and it was done in twenty-seven hours. The only losses were one man wounded and two captured. In General McClellan's report concerning this expedition he says that he did not think it possible for the raiders to re-cross the river, and believed that the capture or destruction of the force was a certainty.

On the hotly contested field of Brandy Station, on June 9, 1863, General Hampton's younger

Lieutenant-Colonel Frank Hampton, slain in the battle of Brandy Station, younger brother of General Hampton.

brother, Lieutenant-Colonel Frank Hampton, of the Second South Carolina Cavalry, was killed, shot through the body while fighting hand to hand with sabre, literally "facing fearful odds." He died leaving every man his friend who had ever known him, and without a private enemy. Here, too, M. C. Butler, then colonel of the same regiment, lost his leg. On another part of the field General Hampton was that day performing brilliant service in many a charge. One of these, a mounted charge against a fine Federal brigade, was said to have been the most hotly contested and magnificent horse encounter of the war, but Hampton's star lighted the path and his sabre cleft the way to victory. As the General dashed to the head of his command to lead them on this occasion, his eyes " snapping fire," as the men used to say, he threw off his overcoat to leave his sword-arm free, and flung it to his son Preston, acting Orderly, a mere boy, who was afterwards killed at Burgess' Mill

"Press" held the coat for a second or two, and then cast it on the ground, exclaiming in soliloquy, "I came here to fight, not carry coats!" and galloping after his father was soon by his side in the charge. The old soldiers who noticed the incident smiled and said, "A chip of the old block." But I must not be led away to linger among the picturesque memories of that attractive period, for my duty is only to recount the story of '64.

In Stuart's march round Hooker's rear and right flank before Gettysburg, Hampton was present as second in command. Without entering at all into the controversy about the effect of this movement on Lee's dispositions at Gettysburg, it is necessary to emphasize the fact that Hampton had no responsibility whatever for the general scope of the march. He carried out his part of the programme in accordance with orders received from Stuart. What the orders were which the latter had received from

Lee, was entirely unknown to anyone except the leader of the expedition, and their exact nature will ever remain a secret buried with the dead. Major McClellan, Stuart's Adjutant-General, says that a long letter from Lee marked "Confidential" was received by him during the night preceding the march, and that, as his General was asleep, he opened the letter and read its contents. Finding these to be important, he awoke Stuart and read the despatch to him, when the latter told him to take charge of it, and went to sleep. Apparently this letter must have been lost during the expedition, or perhaps purposely destroyed to avoid the risk of its falling into the hands of the enemy through some accident or capture. It seems never to have been seen after the night of its receipt, and the only clue to its contents would be the general recollection derived by the adjutant from a hasty perusal. This could establish little, as so much would depend upon the spirit as well as the exact wording of such a communication.

The wagon-train, the bringing of which to Lee's army has been charged with causing the chief delay in the march, was captured within three miles of Washington. It is stated by one of his staff officers that at this time General Hampton advocated a dash on Washington, contending that great mischief could be done and consternation and demoralization produced by such an enterprise, and that, if it proved necessary afterwards, the cavalry could make their way back to Virginia by swimming the river at a practicable point. Of course this proposition was made on its merits at the time, without reference to Lee's orders or to the object of the movement then going on, all of which were unknown to him.

The cavalry, as is well known, only reached its army in time for fighting at Gettysburg, and were too late to be of any service in locating the position of the enemy prior to the battle. Here General Hampton was severely wounded. Five out of the six chambers of his revolver snapped, the pistol having been exposed to much wet weather during the night before, and a Federal succeeded in getting in a sabre cut on the side of his head and forehead, but the one discharge did its work. Afterwards, seeing one of his men hard-pressed, Hampton dashed to his assistance, when the trooper escaped, but the Federal, a good swordsman, turned upon his new adversary. The blood from the wound in the head interfered somewhat with the General's vision, which enabled the Federal to cut under his guard, inflicting a bad wound in the head; but it was the man's last stroke, for Hampton's sabre cleft his head down to the chin, a feat which novels and newspapers airily ascribe to their heroes, but which is rarely performed, and never, except by a stalwart arm and skillful hand. Soon after this a shrapnel struck him on the right thigh, and he was obliged to dismount and permit his wounds to be attended to.

In reviewing Hampton's achievements in his military career, in spite of all the obstacles encountered, it should not be forgotten that the fact of his not being a West Point graduate worked much to his disadvantage. It is beyond argument that the lack of this military training would prove an impediment at first, until practical experience in the field, developing the natural bent, had supplied its place. But, besides this, it would continue long afterwards to stand in the way of promotion. Mr Davis and nearly all the higher officers of the Confederacy were graduates of West Point, and had done much to shape and build up the institution, and they would unavoidably have a feeling about it similar to that entertained by those from universities and colleges concerning their *almæ matres*. Their strong tendency would be, therefore, to have leanings against officers not educated at

West Point, nor even at any other military school. The man who surmounted this very natural prejudice and outranked all the other officers in his branch of the service could have attained his rank only by demonstrating in the field his unquestionable title to such position.

CHAPTER II.

THE CAVALRY IN 1864—SUBSISTENCE, ARMAMENT, HORSES, &C.

MOST people have some general knowledge of the events of the Virginia Campaign of 1864, the most splendid of Lee's achievements. The Federal Army, countless in numbers and unsurpassed in equipment, in early May, commenced its march on Richmond. At the battles in the Wilderness, about Spotsylvania Courthouse, and in minor engagements, it met bloody repulse by "the slender line of gray," and finally suffered decisive defeat at Cold Harbor. During this momentous month of fighting, Grant's losses about equalled the entire number of troops with which

Lee had commenced the campaign. Their relative forces, including reinforcements received by each, compared as one hundred does to forty, or two and a half to one. After Cold Harbor, Grant was compelled to abandon his original plan of capturing Richmond, cross to the south of the James river, and lay siege to Petersburg, strategically an outwork of Richmond. All the while immense Federal reinforcements were being received, but the Confederate ranks could procure few recruits. Yet, in spite of all this, Lee successfully held at bay his antagonist, and the campaign closed in December with Petersburg and Richmond intact.

It matters not what may be one's "politics," nor whether he is born among the snows of the North or under the fervid sun of the South; pluck, fortitude, and military prowess command admiration, apart from creed or clime. Thus it has come about that Lee has won a place in the hearts of all brave men. In America's imperial city overlooking the Hudson, the monument in honor of Grant commemorates the glory of Lee.

The infantry of the Army of Northern Virginia have written "with blood and iron" the record of their campaign of 1864 : the names of their battle-fields are landmarks in history But little is known of the story of the cavalry. And yet they endured privation and death on the lonely picket with only the dead for company ; they went down, rider and horse, in the desperate charge, the hand-to-hand encounter, in unnamed "skirmishes"; dismounted to fight, transformed into infantry, as brave and stubborn as ever grasped the rifle, they fell on fields, styled "cavalry affairs," unknown to fame. May a day come when justice will be done to their memory. The aim of the present attempt is only to recount some facts in the career of their greatest leader.

As most of us in these days know more about streets than strategy, tea than tactics, it might be well to explain what the chief duties of the cavalry were, and their relation to the rest of the army.

During Grant's attempt to break through or flank Lee's lines in the movement on Richmond, it was necessary for the cavalry to discover the points at which the enemy was seeking to concentrate for attack. For this purpose they had to picket all approaches, and report movements, and frequently attack cavalry and drive them in to ascertain the real intentions of the enemy. When ascertained, they had to do their best to defeat them, and failing this, make delay so as to gain time for their own infantry to come up. Frequently, also, they were obliged to fight to mask the movements of their own army. They had also to cover the lines of communication by which supplies were obtained, and to protect Richmond from dashes of raiding-parties. Besides this, they were always on the alert to capture or destroy the enemy's trains and depots;

to threaten and interfere with his lines of communication, and worry him in every conceivable manner. After Grant established the siege of Petersburg, it was necessary for them to supplement the infantry in the trenches protecting the exterior of the flanks, and in resisting attacks. They were thus not only "the eyes and ears of the army," but also its claws: faithful watch-dogs trained to bite, guarding the gateways. The campaign was successfully conducted by Lee, and very able handling of the cavalry was absolutely essential to make such a result possible.

In estimating the merit of the work done by any man, it is proper to take into consideration the means at his disposal for doing it. We must bear in mind, then, not only the number of men under Hampton's command during the campaign of 1864, but also understand about their subsistence, equipment as to arms, supply of horses, and the means of feeding them. I say nothing about deficiency in clothing and shelter, because, though from this they suffered hardships and an increase of mortality, yet the fighting power of these hardy men was probably not impaired by this cause.

The regular rations intended for each man daily consisted of a half pound of bacon or salt pork and a pint of corn meal or flour, but frequently this was reduced by one half, and even the half ration would be, during a great part of the time, curtailed from necessity. The cavalry—because of the nature of their service, their numerous and unexpected movements, and picketing—were more irregularly supplied than the other branches of the service. There could be, usually, no foraging upon the country, for this was precluded by discipline, and, besides, the sections in which they operated were denuded of supplies. Much misapprehension seems to exist about the surroundings of the cavalry compared to those of the infantry. The term "dashing dragoon," applied to the Confederate, was a very inappropriate figure of speech. Any one enlisting under this misconception was likely to have a speedy and rude awakening An instance of this kind will illustrate what is meant. One night the southern bank of the Chickahominy was being picketed, the enemy sociably near on the other side. There had been enough fighting to give every one a stomachful, with little else to do it. So thought a new recruit—tired, hungry, dirty, and generally miserable and disgusted. The malaria seemed visible in the misty exhalations rising from the swamp, and the swarms of mosquitoes were certainly of thoroughbred stock, with whom it was impossible to arrange a *modus vivendi*. To make things more comfortable, two bodies—whether of friend or foe no one knew—had been buried close at hand in such shallow holes as to be partly visible. All night long, from time to time, two dogs, though driven off again and again, would come back and try to scratch away the earth from the corpses, either from affection for the dead or in order to devour them. At length, after a long, gloomy silence, the new recruit said to a comrade:

"Did you ever read Charles O'Malley? It is a blanketty, blanketty blank pack of lies from beginning to end!"

It seems a strange thing, but is nevertheless a fact, that the soldiers who, on the whole, best sustained privations and hardships were not those whose previous habits would be expected to fit them for a rough mode of life. You would look for the dandy to be a hard fighter, for such he has been in all ages. But when it comes to living on half-rancid bacon and husky corn meal, one would suppose him to be at a disadvantage compared with a man brought up among very primitive domestic conditions. Such was not the case—the well-nurtured man would outrough the other. You may, sometimes, have observed the same principle illustrated by your travelling companions, and that those who grumble most about "bed and board" are the ones who have lived most slenderly at home. Shortly after the war the buyer of goods for a country store in a remote section of the South happened to be at dinner in a good hotel in New York. After scanning for a long time in bewilderment the bill of fare with all its French names for familiar dishes, he at last said to the waiter:

"Gim'me bacon."

But, then, he was a connoisseur of bacon. The same fellow, when at breakfast, had ventured upon a codfish ball. After the first mouthful was taken it was returned to his plate with more haste than elegance, and, turning to his companion, he remarked:

"By jimminy! Bill, there's somethin' dead in that tart!"

Beyond the rations above mentioned, there

was not any other food regularly issued until the early autumn, when Hampton had made his celebrated capture of Federal beeves. After that time beef instead of pork was given out occasionally. Now and then in the late autumn, but not at any earlier period of the campaign, a very little sugar and coffee would be dispensed, but so rarely and in such small quantities as to be practically valueless for maintaining health. There were never rations of wine, whiskey, or any alcoholic stimulant, and there was no possibility of procuring anything of the kind from outside sources, even if there had been the money for buying, so the men were "teetotalers" from necessity. At rare intervals a little tobacco in the form of "plugs" was issued, and smoking tobacco could generally be bought comparatively cheap. To make purchases, however, it is necessary to have money, and this must come from "home," for pay-days were like angels' visits, and the currency, even when received, was so depreciated as to have a very limited purchasing power. It will readily be seen what a great disadvantage the Army of Northern Virginia labored under, fighting on such slender subsistence, compared to the amply fed and well cared for Army of the Potomac. It is a grave question how far this condition of affairs was unavoidable and how far it was due to lack of good management in the Departments at Richmond, and to want of zeal in the Quartermasters and Commissaries, and their underlings at depots and with wagon-trains. If the army could have been properly supplied merely with sound bacon and corn meal or flour, these rations would have been sufficient to maintain its physical strength and efficiency and to have prevented much mortality from wounds and sickness, which proved fatal because of the depleted condition of the poor fellows. Certain it is that the bravest, most

The Battle of Brandy Station, Culpeper County, Va., June 9, 1863.

energetic, and ambitious men were to be found at the front, where were danger, glory, and promotion, and also the self-respecting satisfaction earned by well-performed duty, whereas "bomb-proofs" were greatly in demand by persons, as a rule, of an inferior grade, content to be non-combatants. This may and probably does account in a measure for less able conduct of the Quartermaster Department and the consequent privations of the troops. After the continuous fighting of a month from the Wilderness to Cold Harbor, it was desired by Lee to have the rations of the men, temporarily at least, increased somewhat, and coffee or some other stimulant issued, to bring up the physical condition, but the Department stated it was impossible to do this.

In armament the cavalry were sorely overmatched by their opponents. Lee's Infantry were armed with muzzle-loaders, but then the Federal Infantry used similar weapons, and therefore they were on the same footing in this respect. Hampton's Cavalry generally possessed only muzzle-loaders. The regiments from the Carolinas and Georgia had no breech-loaders at all. It is true some of the Virginia regiments were provided with Sharp's breech-loading carbines (single-shooters), but there were comparatively few. On this point General Rosser writes: "Our cavalry had no breech-loading arms, except those captured, and with these the 'Laurel Brigade' was pretty well supplied. Nearly all my men were armed with captured arms, and supplied with captured saddles, bridles, and halters." But General Rosser's Brigade had been detached for service in the Valley, and had therefore enjoyed exceptional opportunities for thus equipping itself, as the Federal armies there had been throughout the war in a measure an adjunct to the Confederate Ordnance Department. The repeating carbines captured could not be utilized during the campaign of 1864 for lack of ammunition, because the Confederate work-shops were unable, at that time, to manufacture the metallic cartridges. They learned to do this late in the autumn, and could have furnished them for the next campaign. And by that time, too, they would have been able to supply breech-loaders of their own manufacture; some were already made and in the arsenal in Columbia, S. C., when the city was burned by Sherman, where were also produced the heavy, long, straight, double-edged swords, very serviceable and crusader-like, with cross-hilt. The Sharp's carbines captured were at best only single-shooters, and besides the cartridges were of paper and easily injured by wear in the boxes and by weather In August, 1864, an order was issued taking away from the men any captured magazine rifles in their possession, because the impossibility of procuring fresh supplies of cartridges would make them useless at critical moments. Hampton's Cavalry, therefore, as a rule, had only muzzle-loaders. These were mostly Enfield rifles, but many of them less serviceable weapons, and not a few mere artillery carbines, little better than cross-bows. Grant's Cavalry, on the other hand, were provided with breech-loading carbines, and largely with magazine rifles, chiefly Spencer's. The muzzle-loader is a thing of the past, and therefore hardly known to this generation, except by name, being almost as unfamiliar as the Queen Anne flint-lock musket. It is therefore difficult to appreciate the terrible disadvantages the Confederate Cavalry labored under in this matter. To load the Enfield was slow work at best, the difficulty greatly increasing as it became foul from repeated discharges. It could not well be loaded by a man lying down on the ground behind cover, thus necessitating greater exposure of the person in fighting. The cartridges, being of paper, were liable to injury by dampness and rain, and the rifles often would miss fire and cause much delay and trouble. The breech-loading carbines and magazine rifles were free from all these drawbacks, besides possessing rapid-firing power, and troops armed with them ought to have been equal to at least double their number carrying only muzzle-loaders. In respect to revolvers, Hampton's men were also sadly deficient, a considerable percentage being without them, whilst their enemy was amply provided. But not only were the rifles inferior in quality, but they were also insufficient in number to equip all the men. It appears from the "Armament Report of the Cavalry Corps, December 15, 1864," that the number of men in the command was then 5,552, of whom 1,100 were unarmed, and 925 did not have long-range guns, and a large proportion were without revolvers. This report was of course intended to apply only to the Government property issued to the men, and not to personal weapons, which, being private property, would not be returned in the schedule. The deplorable deficiency in arms was not caused by any fault of the Ordnance Department of the Confederate Government, which, on the contrary, was ably managed, and did good work in proportion to its available resources. The stringent blockade, hampering imports, and the paucity of work-shops and mechanics, and financial straits, were responsible for this. General Hampton was unceasingly endeavoring to minimize the difficulty by urgent correspondence with the Department, by captures, and by efforts to import arms. The powder, at least, was always good, which was largely due to the skill and energy of Colonel Raines, detailed to superintend the Powder Works of Augusta, Ga. When he died recently it was a request in his will that his body should be wrapped in a Confederate flag, which he had provided for the purpose, and buried on the site of his old works.

But the horse supply was the weakest point of all in the organization of the cavalry. When a man enlisted he brought with him his own mount. If the horse was killed in action, he would be entitled by law to compensation, but this was nominal, not real, for, if he ever received the money at all, it would be at a fixed valuation for the horse in depreciated currency equivalent to only a small fraction of the actual value of the animal. If the horse was lost or disabled by wear and tear or disease, he received no compensation at all. In any case, if dismounted, he must provide himself with another horse, or be transferred into some other branch of the service. Good men were often lost to the cavalry by being unable to buy a fresh mount. Where the trooper could manage to afford to purchase another animal, it was necessary to give him a furlough to go home for this purpose, obtain his mount, and bring him back to the command. And so the disablement of a horse meant either the elimination of a man from the force altogether, or at least his absence on furlough for a long time, and this would, of course, most frequently occur when the work was hardest and men most needed. This feature was the fatal defect of the system, and it may well be wondered how, in these circumstances, the cavalry was kept in existence at all. The entire system, however, is not to be condemned because of this vital fault, for it possesses many merits, and it may be necessary to utilize it again on a large scale in some future wars, but it is essential that the supply of fresh horses should be provided for when those originally furnished by the troopers are worn out. In raising cavalry in this way many important advantages are gained. Better men and better horses are obtained on the average. The recruits will be largely composed of substantial countrymen who can ride and shoot and understand the care of horses, with a fair sprinkling of young fellows from towns who are fond of horses and are quick to acquire the discipline of a soldier. Though, according to law, captured horses became the property of the Government and not of the men in the command taking them, yet, after a time, unwritten law largely overrode this red tape, and captured mounts would be retained by the captors in lieu of their own dead or unserviceable animals. General Thomas L. Rosser says in this connection:

"I often went into battle or on a raid with one-third at least of my men dismounted, and generally succeeded in mounting them from captures."

The daily forage ordered to be issued for the horses, *when practicable*, was ten pounds, equal to about five and three-fourth quarts of corn (maize) and ten pounds of long forage for each animal; but this quantity was, in point of fact, never given out, because it could not be procured. Often only five pounds of corn per horse and no long forage would be issued, and not infrequently only two and one-half pounds. Sometimes there would be no corn at all, and merely scant rations of hay, or even straw. Not infrequently the only subsistence would be unthreshed wheat. The privations were most severe during the active period of the campaign, but even when that was ended the lack of forage was keenly felt. A more distressing sight than to witness the daily deterioration of the horses under this treatment can hardly be imagined. The deprivation of grain is very bad for them, but the absence of long forage is worse; the animal's digestion becoming so completely upset by this that even with a sufficiency of corn he would not derive the normal benefit from it. The unsatisfied craving for long forage produces a morbid appetite, and the horse will then greedily seize and swallow almost anything to distend the stomach. Where a camp had been located for a few days one would notice the trees to which the horses had been fastened stripped of bark from the ground to as high up as the animals could reach, and where the place was occupied for a week or two many of the smaller trees would be eaten entirely away. Empty bags, scraps of paper, and similar things would often be voraciously devoured. Unfortunately the supply of long forage was much less in proportion than that of corn. Even in summer there were very few opportunities for grazing, and in the autumn and winter none. All this was lamentable in a humane point of view and extremely painful to those fond of their horses, but it was also an immense injury to the efficiency of the cavalry. General Hampton fully appreciated the vast importance of bettering the food supply for the horses, and his efforts in this direction were most energetic and untiring, and every possible expedient which his wide and life-long experience of the subject could suggest was put in practice. No doubt the department of the Confederate Government charged with attending to this subject had, at that time, very great difficulties to grapple with.

Another drawback to the efficiency of the cavalry was the difficulty of obtaining horseshoes, and an unshod horse meant, for the time being, the loss in action of one sabre and one rifle.

Of course the disparity of relative numbers was, of all, the most serious disadvantage to the Confederates. It has been, throughout this narrative, the conscientious intention to report correctly the military results attained and the actual numbers engaged and losses sustained. For this purpose the "Records of Union and Confederate Armies," published by the War Department from original or authenticated documents, are invaluable, but they are not infallible. Official reports are frequently more or less colored by the interest or prejudices of the officer making them. As to numbers, losses, prisoners, and recruits there is room in these "Records" for serious mistakes without any intention of deception, and the documents themselves sometimes contain internal evidence of this. In keeping accounts involving returns of vast numbers daily changing, it would be too much to expect uniform accuracy, but, besides accidental inaccuracies, documents at headquarters and in the wagons were occasionally lost or captured. This occurred most frequently from May to September, 1864, often with the infantry, but still more commonly with the cavalry, because of the more active nature and varied vicissitudes of that service. Where papers containing the data of corps, divisions, brigades, or parts of them are thus lost, accuracy cannot be expected from returns made up afterwards in the absence of such data. It would be like the effort of a banker to establish the previous debits and credits of his accounts with his customers after he had lost all of his books in a fire. Moreover the cavalry on both sides, for days together, had more pressing business to attend to than bookkeeping, which would be relegated to more convenient occasions. As instances of the loss of or inability to obtain data, the following may be cited. General Meade endorses on the report of the Army of the Potomac of June 30, 1864:

"The last trimonthly report previously rendered was for April 30th. In consequence of the movements of the troops between the dates mentioned and the absence of all facilities for the preparation of the stated trimonthly reports, it was found altogether impracticable to render such reports when due."

On the returns of the Army of the Potomac for July 31, 1864, there is an endorsement stating that the records of the First and Third Divisions of Cavalry had been "lost or captured," and therefore could not be given.

Preparing for the field. From many of the humbler homes came many of the finest soldiers.

CHAPTER III.

POSITION OF THE ARMIES BEFORE THE OPENING OF THE CAMPAIGN OF 1864—SURPRISE OF KILPATRICK'S FORCE—DAHLGREN RAID.

MAJOR-GENERAL J. E. B. STUART, commanding the cavalry of the Army of Northern Virginia, was mortally wounded on May 11, 1864, and, by his death on the following day, Hampton became ranking Major-General of the command. This narrative, strictly speaking, should commence at that date, but a clearer understanding of the situation will be arrived at by a brief reference to some occurrences which preceded May 11th.

During the winter of 1863-'64 General Hampton, with headquarters at Milford, had two brigades of his division—Butler's and Gorden's—stationed near Fredericksburg, about sixty miles north of Richmond, picketing the Rapidan and Rappahannock rivers, on the right of the army. The other brigade of the division—Rosser's—had been ordered to the Shenandoah Valley in December. The two brigades mentioned numbered together seven hundred and nineteen, "present for duty and with serviceable horses," by the field return for February 28th. The infantry occupied, for about twenty miles, the southern bank of the Rapidan, extending on the left to near Orange Courthouse, and Meade's army was some ten miles to the north of their centre.

On February 29th occured what may be considered the first movement in the cavalry campaign of 1864. On that morning General Hampton received information from a scout that the Federal infantry were supposed to be moving, and that Kilpatrick was in motion with his cavalry division.

This information was correct as to Kilpatrick, but the infantry movements as well as the cavalry demonstration around the left flank were merely feints, intended to distract attention from the real object in view. Kilpatrick had received orders to march with a force of four thousand men, and with about this number and six pieces of horse artillery he started on his expedition on Sunday evening, February 28th. The purpose was to dash round the right flank of Lee's army and capture Richmond, which had only a feeble garrison, consisting largely of home guards. His force was composed of men selected from all of the three divisions of the corps. Pleasanton, then commanding the Federal cavalry, speaks of them as "picked men," and says that, for this reason, their absence seriously impaired the efficiency of all his three divisions. Probably there were also some of the "household troops," as General Meade used to style men detailed to serve around army headquarters. Colonel Dahlgren led the advance with four hundred and sixty men. The plan was for him to press forward, unencumbered with wagons, cross the James river, seize the bridge and be ready to attack Richmond from the south side in co-operation with Kilpatrick, who counted upon reaching the northern side by Tuesday morning. The expedition accordingly quietly crossed the Rapidan at Ely's ford during Sunday night, having captured or killed the whole picket from Butler's brigade—fourteen men and an officer—and set out on their race for Richmond, some fifty miles in a straight line to the southward. Kilpatrick duly reached the neighborhood of Richmond on Tuesday about midday, but Dahlgren had not been able to keep his appointment. Kilpatrick made a feeble attack upon the outworks of Richmond, but drew off early in the evening and went into camp near Atlee's station, intending to renew his attempt upon the city in the morning, by which time he hoped

Dahlgren would be in position, or would have joined him.

Meantime, as soon as he had ascertained the direction taken by the raiders, Hampton started energetically in pursuit. His force consisted of three hundred and six troopers from the First and Second North Carolina regiments, of Gorden's brigade, and Hart's battery of horse artillery—these being all the men that could be spared without denuding the picket posts. Sunday night had been a beautiful, bright, moonlight evening, mild and spring-like, so much so that a signal-corps officer, with an unpronounceable Sclavonic name, attached to Dahlgren's band, in his official report moralizes most edifyingly upon the calm of nature being in striking contrast with the angry passions of man, and a little latter on becomes eloquent over the beauty of a bonfire made by buildings burned. But the weather suddenly changed completely, and on Tuesday there was a severe storm, accompanied by snow and sleet, and the night closed in black as ink, cold and wet. Towards ten o'clock Hampton made out the camp-fires of the enemy—one portion near Atlee's station, about ten miles north of Richmond, and the others just back of it. He decided at once to attack the brigade nearest the station, and set his men in motion in that direction, with orders when the enemy's pickets were met not to return their fire. When this occurred he dismounted one hundred of his men, supporting them with the remainder mounted, and advanced steadily upon Kilpatrick's camp, whilst two pieces of artillery were opened upon it at short range. At first a stout resistance was encountered from the brigade attacked, but Hampton dashed in and carried the camp at a rush. About one hundred prisoners were captured, the rest making off in the darkness, leaving many horses. Arms, rations, and clothing were found scattered about.

Until they struck the camp itself the advance of Hampton's men had been made in as noiseless a manner as practicable, so as to effect a surprise, but when the charge took place the men tried to create all the noise possible, because this would produce the impression of greater numbers. The "rebel yell," derived from the inspiring view-halloo of the hunting field, could express, on fitting occasions, an intensity of fierceness quite upsetting to the nerves.

Meantime General Kilpatrick, with the brigades camped in the rear, "in guarded tent," like the Turk of old, was snugly snoozing in warm blankets regardless of the pitiless storm without, and "was dreaming of the hour" when he would sack Richmond and become the next President. He "woke," not "to die 'mid flame and smoke," nor "death-shots falling thick and fast," but to leap upon his horse in hot haste and gallop away into the darkness, followed by his intact brigades, forgetting to take with him a loaded wagon, with horses hitched, and a caisson of ammunition, and having experienced a very "unpleasant quarter of an hour"

In consequence of the extreme darkness Hampton could not take up the pursuit until daylight. In the interim the victors made bold to use the fires, provisions, coffee, and other "home comforts" left behind by their departed hosts.

Kilpatrick says in his official report, that after his involuntary night march he reached Old Church, where he rested until one o'clock P M. the next day, but hearing that Hampton was "after him," as he expresses it, and that it was he, with "a large force of mounted infantry and cavalry and four pieces of artillery" who had attacked him the night before, he "decided to move by the nearest route to General Butler's lines at New Kent Courthouse." It should be remembered that "the large force" numbered, after deducting necessary details for scouts and pickets, less than three hundred men.

After resting and receiving reinforcements at Yorktown, Kilpatrick essayed to force his way back to his own army, but Hampton barred the way, having somewhat increased his force by that time. And so it turned out that Kilpatrick was cut off from Meade's army, to which he belonged, and, compelled to seek refuge in General Butler's bosom, became "bottled up," thus setting an example soon followed by Butler His losses, according to Federal returns, were only 340. His friends were obliged to send steamers to Yorktown to bring him back to his army, where, as Pleasanton states, the absence of his "picked men" and the "household troops" was severely felt. This seems rather a droll ending for the affair. Old Ben Butler, too, had shortly before this got up an expedition with similar purpose against Richmond, which, like all his sensational attempts at war, had come to speedy grief.

Dahlgren had endeavored to carry out his

part of the programme. After burning some mills, barns, and other private property, encountering no organized resistance, he had tried to cross the James river, about twenty miles above Richmond, but had not succeeded in effecting this. Suspecting that a negro boy, whom he had employed as guide, was deceiving him about the ford, he hanged the poor creature. A party of five or six of his scouts rode up to a country house near by. On the piazza were two young men, soldiers on furlough, and the ladies of the family The young people were not aware of raiders being in the neighborhood, and were so busy chatting together they did not perceive the intruders until they were almost among them. Then, quick as thought, the two men ran through the hall, escaped by the back door, rushed to the stable, mounted, and galloped away into the fields in the rear. Meantime the raiders demanded that the ladies should tell them where the men were, whom they had seen leaving, and also required to be informed of the road to the nearest river-ford. This being refused, they threatened their lives, and levelled cocked pistols at their heads, but did not succeed in extorting any information from these brave Virginia girls. Soon the two young men, discovering that the Federals numbered only five or six, came dashing round the corner of the house, yelling as if leading a charge, and chased them away with their pistols. One, the most insolent of the gang, endeavored to escape by making a short cut across the lawn to the gate on the main road. On his way was a deep excavation, which had once been an ice-house, but which had gone to ruin, and was then concealed by *debris* and grass. Into this the rider and horse, at full speed, fell. Both were found there quite dead, their necks broken, and there they lie buried now. It is not surprising that these girls should always have believed the arm of the Great Avenger had been present with them. Despairing of crossing the river, Dahlgren made a fruitless ride to the outskirts of Richmond, but drew off without accomplishing anything Hearing that Hampton had driven off Kilpatrick, and was interposed between him and his friends, he seemed to lose his head, and blindly endeavored to escape. His command became divided in the darkness, and he with a part of it was encountered by an irregular band made up of citizens and a few soldiers on furlough, and thus met his death, and those accompanying him shared his fate or became prisoners. On his body was found a note-book and papers containing memoranda, and his intended programme after capturing Richmond, which included the burning of the city and the assassination of the Confederate President, proceedings which would have been in violation of the laws of civilized warfare. It is probable that from this attempt was suggested

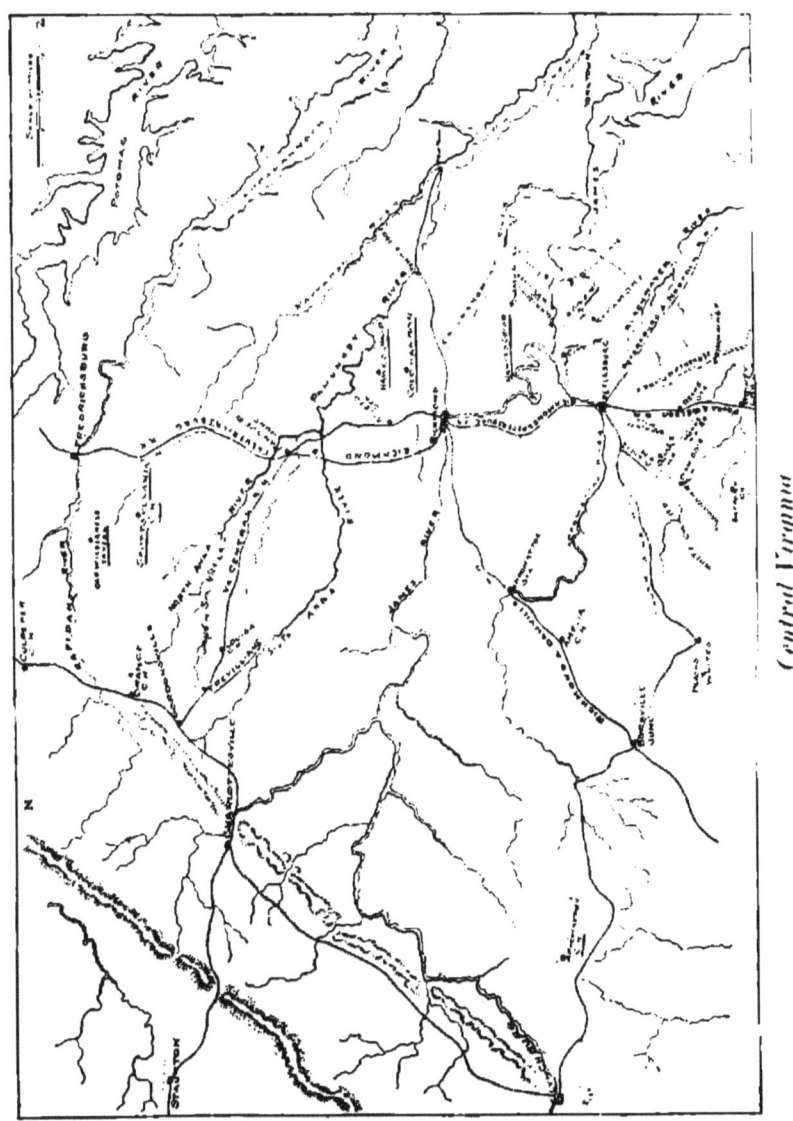
Central Virginia

the idea of the equally abhorrent crime of which Lincoln was the victim. The one atrocity begot the other. Naturally enough friends of Dahlgren tried to discredit the evidence against him, but unfortunately the facts speak for themselves.

As to the documentary evidence against Dahlgren, General Hampton says

"As the authenticity of these papers has been denied, it may not be out of place for me to state here what I know regarding them. As already said, I followed Kilpatrick, when he retreated, and I halted on the night of the 2d of March near the house of Dr. Braxton, and not far from that of Mr. Lewis Washington. I remained during the night at the house of the former, and moving off at a very early hour the next morning I met Mr. Washington, who asked me if I had seen a courier who was in search of me. Replying to him in the negative, he informed me that this courier had stayed at his house the night previous, and had exhibited to him the note-book of Dahlgren, in which he read the diabolical plan, which was subsequently made public. The details of this plan, as stated to me by Mr. Washington, were precisely similar to those published; so, unless the parties who killed Dahlgren, or the courier who bore the despatches on to Richmond on not finding me, wrote the orders and memoranda in the captured note-book, a supposition entirely incredible, there can be no shadow of a doubt that Dahlgren was the originator of a plot to burn and sack Richmond, and to assassinate the President of the Southern Confederacy."

For his services in driving away Kilpatrick, Hampton received the thanks of Major-General Elzey, as the following extract from General Orders will show.

"G. O. No. 10, Headq'rs Department of Richmond, March 8, 1864.

" The Major-General commanding begs leave to tender to Major-General Hampton and his command his sincere thanks for their co-operation in following up the enemy, and their gallant assault upon his camp at Atlee's station on Tuesday night, in which the enemy's entire force was stampeded and completely routed, leaving in the hands of Gen. Hampton many prisoners and horses."

This attack on Kilpatrick, considering the odds, was certainly one of the boldest ever made, but it was not done in a spirit of wild adventure or dare-devil recklessness, but, on the contrary, was sagaciously planned and coolly executed, as the best available means for driving off the raid from Richmond.

CHAPTER IV

REORGANIZATION OF HAMPTON'S DIVISION—COMMENCEMENT OF THE CAMPAIGN—WILDERNESS—SHERIDAN'S RICHMOND RAID—DEATH OF STUART—HAMPTON IN COMMAND—COMPOSITION AND NUMBERS OF THE CORPS—SHERIDAN'S CORPS, AND NUMBER OF MEN—HAWES' SHOP—MATADEQUIN CREEK—ASHLAND—COLD HARBOR.

AFTER the events just related, it was expected there would be comparative quiet until the opening of the spring campaign by the infantry. General Hampton, therefore, availed himself of this opportunity to accept, for a short time, the leave of absence which had been tendered him some time previously. His chief object in this was to return to South Carolina to superintend the transfer to Virginia of the Fourth, Fifth, and Sixth regiments of South Carolina cavalry, who would relieve the First and Second South Carolina cavalry then in Virginia, and thus permit the latter to return home to recruit. This, it was hoped, would bring nearly 2,400 fresh men and horses to Hampton's division in place of the depleted regiments mentioned. It had been decided to do this after his repeated and urgent requests to the War Department, and at the recommendation of General Lee. It had also been arranged to recruit, as far as practicable, with men and horses the other regiments of his division, but, in regard to these, changes were made which will be explained later on. It was absolutely necessary to increase the numerical strength of his command, if it was to be of any material service in the coming campaign.

On May 2d General Hampton returned to his headquarters at Milford, and reported to

General Stuart, commanding the corps. He officially stated his effective force then to be only 673 men. On May 5th his division was reorganized, Gorden's brigade being transferred from it. After that it consisted of Rosser's, Young's, and Butler's brigades, the latter to be made up of the three South Carolina regiments just referred to, which were coming from home.

On May 4th the Army of the Potomac commenced to move, and thus was begun the campaign of 1864. A splendid army it was. All that money could effect in creating and perfecting an armed force, with the resources of the whole world at hand to draw from, had been accomplished. The winter had been spent in the camps north of the Rapidan industriously preparing, organizing, drilling—and this was the result. The soldiers, recruited from every race the sun shines upon, were better cared for, clothed, and fed than most of them had been when at home, and, in numbers and equipment, far surpassed any army that had ever been mustered on American soil. By count there were about one hundred and fifty thousand of all arms, including those detailed to the Quartermaster Department, and nearly fifty thousand of reinforcements were destined to join them during the next four weeks. These are "official" figures, but how many more may have been really there within that horrible month no one can know, for, in the continuous smash of battle and resulting disorganization, accounts for receipts and consumption of "food for gunpowder" could not be accurately kept, and records must be often made up by "forced balances."

General Meade had struck his gorgeous headquarters tent at Culpeper and unfurled his beautiful silken flag, embroidered in silver and gold, at much cost of "greenbacks," suggesting, as General Grant sarcastically remarked in his downright way, the magnificence of the conquerors of imperial Rome. An array of horsemen, some sixteen thousand strong, clattered in the advance, brilliant in all the bravery of handsome uniforms and glittering steel; much larger in numbers and better mounted and accoutered than any cavalry the army had ever before possessed. Then marched the infantry, the sunlight flashing from their rifle-barrels, in high heart and splendid physique, with hundreds of brilliant standards waving, the air filled with the strains of martial music and the tramp of armed men. The rumble of the wheels of the artillery swelled into a volume of sound resembling distant thunder, as well it might, for never before since man gave proof of his kinship to Cain by making gunpowder had so many guns of such calibre been attached to any army. Wagon-trains—consisting of thousands, which, in a single line, would have stretched over sixty miles in length, conveying ample and luxurious rations and provision for sick and wounded, and swarms of camp followers of both sexes—like flies following a carcass—brought up the rear.

Thus they crossed the Rapidan to the southward, filling all the roads with dense masses of moving blue like swollen tributaries to some great river, and overflowing into the open spaces and fields as spring streams will inundate the meadows. It is not to be wondered at that some who watched the spectacle from an overlooking height could almost fancy they were witnessing one of those vast migrations of nations which, it is believed, occurred in prehistoric times, when—set in motion by stress of changed climate and impoverished soil, or overcrowding of the maternal hive—they wandered off by thousands and thousands in search of abiding places in more favored climes. And this migration, too, was from the North, hardly as yet released from the ice-grip, into the genial

Southern lands—to Virginia, smiling in the spring sunshine, wreathed with verdure and flowers, well styled the "Virgin Queen."

In this manner—in all the "pomp and circumstance of war"—the Army of the Potomac proceeded on its way into the Wilderness, there to encounter disaster and defeat, and narrowly to escape entire destruction; to lose within thirty days considerably more than sixty thousand of its best and bravest.

And what barrier existed against this mighty tidal wave of conquest? Merely "a slender line of gray"—unpaid, ill-fed, ragged men. True; but that "line," however "slender," though in numbers hardly equal to two-fifths of its enemy, was composed of the veterans of the Army of Northern Virginia—Americans tried and true, mostly descendants of the British race, whose ancestors had thrown off only the English Crown and titles, but retained all else—the dearly-loved traditions, laws, and liberty; and these had, mingled in their veins, the blood of fiery Cavalier and fighting Roundhead, deriving from each strain its best qualities. And there were not wanting the offspring of that people true to their faith, who followed the white plume of Navarre at Ivry. To all such men comes from their birth facility of military organization and skill with weapons, and to their hearts the word "liberty" always sounds like a bugle-blast. As for the cavalry they were chiefly country-bred, hardy in habits, horsemen from the cradle, and much leavened with the love of field-sports; from the stirring cries of the hunting-field and the mad gallop after the hounds it was an easy transition to the Confederate battle-yell and the dashing, fierce, furious charge. Above all this, that "slender line" was imbubed with almost superhuman strength by the genius and moral power of Lee.

The writer will venture to make a short digression here to relate an incident occurring during the autumn of 1863, which will far better illustrate than any words of his can do, the nature of the leader and of the army confronting Grant in 1864. The exact date, the names of persons, and the locality are omitted for obvious reasons. It is to be feared that the interpretation of this anecdote will not be clear to many a worthy well-to-do citizen, whose combative experiences have been confined to the battles between "bulls" and "bears," whose greatest personal peril has been incurred in dodging bicycles and trolley-cars, whose privations have consisted of dinners not quite *comme il faut*, and whose patriotism is a love for "the old flag and an appropriation." But the women will comprehend it, however white their hands or delicate their nurture.

A commander of a considerable force of Confederate infantry had, by an error of judgment but with the best intentions, made a movement which placed his troops at a great disadvantage and cost fruitlessly much precious blood. As they would have said in those days, he "butted his head against a stone wall." General Lee came upon the scene just then—calm, dignified, and grand ; the personification of mind versus matter. The lines were restored and affairs set right. The infantry officer whose blunder had wrought all this mischief was a gallant and devoted soldier, and his heart was wrung with grief as he looked upon the stiff and stark and the poor fellows writhing with their wounds. He rode up and was about to make some explanation of the mistake, but Lee interrupted him very gently, saying :

"Well, well, General ! bury your poor dead !"

Only those few simple words, but they expressed a pathos that is indescribable. Many dead lay there, and far too many wounded. These latter saw their loved General's look, and some heard his words, and these tried to cheer from their dying throats, and the cry was taken up by others more distant, until at length the very sky shook with the swelling battle-yell of the army. It was magnificent, because it signified the supreme height to which human hearts can reach in love, loyalty, and absolute trust; and surely never since darkness brooded over the face of the waters did a more acceptable anthem ascend to the throne of the Most High.

The Army of the Potomac during its career had served under many different leaders. Meade was now nominally at its head on this momentous 4th of May, but Grant, in fact, exercised personal control and direction. In the cavalry also an important change had occurred since the close of the last campaign. General Pleasanton, during the previous year, had commanded and had much increased the efficiency of this branch of the service. He had consolidated into a corps of three divisions a force which before that had been composed of disconnected regiments and brigades. But his relations with Meade became strained and he felt compelled to resign. Then Grant and Hallet consulted together and selected Sheridan, who was brought from the West to lead the cavalry of the Army of the Potomac, and took command on April 5th. He it was who was destined to be pitted against Hampton in the coming campaign. Some distinction had been gained by him in the West, but chiefly at the head of an infantry division. He happened to have been born in New York, but both his parents, less than a year previous to his birth, had emigrated from Ireland, and he was, therefore, as much an Irishman in racial characteristics as if a native of Cork. From this race has come, during modern times, much raw material for soldiers of fortune, and most of them have shown good fighting qualities. Sheridan was no exception to this rule. Of humble parentage, his early education had been meagre, but he entered West Point from Ohio and graduated in 1853, thirty-fifth in a class of fifty-two members. From this time to his death he lived in the army. When assigned to the command of the cavalry corps of the Army of the Potomac he was thirty-three years of age, and in personal appearance very far from imposing.

On May 7th, in pursuance of orders, General Hampton reached Shady Grove, and, under Stuart, took part in the fighting with the Federal cavalry on that flank. On May 8th Grant, having suffered bloody repulse in the Wilderness fights of the three preceding days, commenced to make a rush to his left to turn Lee's right flank. Time was of vital importance, for Lee must arrive first at the point of attack, and thus be able to confront his antagonist. So the Federal cavalry tried their utmost to clear the roads for their infantry, and the watch-dogs of Lee assailed them for delay, and thus Hampton was again engaged. On May 9th and 10th he was encountering the enemy's infantry, and in the heavy fighting of the 12th his artillery did good service. On every day, from the commencement of the campaign to the battle of Cold Harbor, the cavalry were engaged, always striving their utmost to delay the forward march of the Federal columns, and always forced to fall back gradually before their larger numbers. This is a sort of service which is the hardest that can be put upon troops, for they know full well each morning that the struggle is, for them, a hopeless one, and yet that they must encounter it day after day, forced back always, but disputing every inch. Troops that can endure this, undemoralized, are veterans tried and true, and such cannot be bought for bounties.

On May 9th Sheridan made a detour round Lee's right flank and marched in the direction of Richmond. He had detached a portion of his command to remain with the infantry, but had with him the remainder of his three divisions, numbering over nine thousand men, and seven batteries of horse artillery accompanied them. Stuart started in pursuit, his force being about one-third the strength of that of Sheridan, and by hard riding he interposed himself between the raiders and Richmond, having detached General Gorden, with his very small brigade, formerly of Hampton's division, to attack their rear. On May 11th a severe fight ensued at Yellow Tavern, nine miles from Richmond, during which, after many hours, Stuart's line was broken through by force of numbers. He himself was mortally wounded and died the following day. Thus fell a gallant, devoted soldier and a lovable man. His personal dash was splendid and his handling of mounted cavalry spirited. The daring raids and adventurous expeditions conducted by him are captivating to the imagination and surround his memory with romantic associations. Brigadier-General Gorden, too, an excellent officer, lost his life in this unequal contest, fighting stoutly in the front, as was his wont.

Sheridan, having succeeded in passing through Stuart's line, proceeded to the fortifications of Richmond, where he made an attack and was repulsed. The garrison consisted, to a great extent, of citizen soldiers, supplemented by some troops which General Bragg, commanding the defences, brought up from below Richmond, and was, therefore, not a very formidable body, either in numbers or quality However, Sheridan gave up the attempt to capture the city and returned to his infantry, arriving there on May 25th. His losses in this expedition, according to Federal returns, were six hundred and twenty-five.

The results accomplished by this raid amounted to very little of military value. The appearance of Federal cavalry behind the lines caused the withdrawal from Lee of no infantry, and of only about one-third of the number of troopers comprised in Sheridan's force; in other words, it required three of his men to neutralize one of the cavalry of the Army of Northern Virginia. The public stores burnt, and the railroads only slightly and temporarily interfered with, did not at all diminish the efficiency of the troops then operating against Grant. Nether did the destruction of private property damage anyone but the individual sufferers, and, indeed, it was of benefit rather than injury to the Confederate cause, on account of the exasperation of feeling thus engendered. The attack on Richmond proved a failure, and caused no diversion in any other direction. It is true Stuart was killed, but that can hardly be called a "result," for we do not wage war, like Indians, for human scalps, but only to obtain military ends.

What, then, was the purpose of this expedition? It has been said that one object was to draw off cavalry from Lee, and thus render more easy Grant's flanking movements, but, as remarked above, this was a three-for-one "exchange." The attack on Richmond was so feeble that *it* could hardly have been the objective point. One writer has said the chief purpose of the march was to recruit the horses, but a hard raid in a country swept of supplies would certainly be a strange method, and surely no commander would, at a critical juncture, separate his cavalry from his infantry for such an inadequate reason. The true explanation of the proceeding probably is, that Grant overconfidently expected to hammer to pieces Lee's columns at Spotsylvania, and placed Sheridan in the rear to pulverize the fragments. Thus to denude the army of cavalry would seem to have been a frightful risk, and might well have ended the war in exactly an opposite manner to that intended.

By the death of Major-General J. E. B. Stuart on May 12th, Hampton, as senior Major-General, became commander of the cavalry of the Army of Northern Virginia. He was then forty-six years of age. Of impressive personal appearance—full-bearded, tall, erect, and massive; a horseman from life-long habit and natural aptitude—he looked a grand military chieftain. The cavalry of that army constituted a corps. There were at that time three divisions—the First consisting of M. C. Butler's brigade, the Fourth, Fifth, and Sixth South Carolina, Young's brigade, Cobb's Legion, Phillips' Legion, Jeff. Davis Legion, Seventh Georgia regiment, Millens' battalion, and Lewis' battalion, Thomas L. Rosser's brigade, Seventh, Eleventh, and Twelfth Virginia, and White's battalion. This division was commanded by Major-General Hampton. The Second division was made up of Wickham's brigade, First, Second, Third, and Fourth Vir-

ginia and Lomax's brigade, Fifth, Sixth, and Fifteenth Virginia. Major-General Fitzhugh Lee commanded this division. The Third division was composed of Gorden's brigade, First, Second, Third, and Fifth North Carolina and Chambliss' brigade, Ninth, Tenth, and Thirteenth Virginia. This division was under Major-General W H. F Lee.

General Fitzhugh Lee was a nephew and General W H. F Lee, a son of Robert E. Lee, and both were graduates of West Point.

When General Hampton took command after May 12, 1864, the three divisions were composed as above stated, but all the regiments were not present. The three regiments of Butler's brigade had not yet reached Virginia, nor the larger part of Young's brigade, nor two regiments of Gorden's brigade. The regiments not present on May 12th reported at different dates during the rest of the month. The number of effective men present for duty with serviceable horses never exceeded, at any time during the campaign, seven thousand as a maximum. This statement is confirmed by General Hampton. The force was undergoing constant reduction by dismounts, caused by broken-down horses as well as by casualties, whilst new recruits were necessarily few, and, therefore, this maximum existed for only a moment, so to speak. Gary's brigade—consisting of the Hampton Legion (ten companies), Seventh South Carolina Cavalry and Twenty-sixth Virginia cavalry—was not attached to the corps, but belonged to the Richmond-defence force, and operated only north of the James river

The cavalry of Sheridan consisted also of three divisions, styled First, Second, and Third, commanded by Generals Torbert, Gregg, and Wilson—ranking in the order named. The number of brigades comprised in the corps was seven and the number of regiments thirty. By the "abstract of the tri-monthly return of the Army of the Potomac for April 30, 1864," the number of officers and men then "present for duty" in the cavalry corps was fifteen thousand eight hundred and twenty-five, and "serviceable horses" fifteen thousand and thirty-six. Their numerical strength was, therefore, at that time considerably more than double the maximum of Hampton's force, and very far more than double its average. Sheridan's troops were admirably clothed, equipped, armed, and fed, and were kept mounted by fresh supplies of horses, and the ranks constantly replenished with new recruits. Their arms consisted of breech-loaders (chiefly Spencer and Hall magazine rifles of the best kind, using metallic cartridges), revolvers, and sabres. The sad contrast to this presented by Hampton's command in food, armament, horses, and forage has been pointed out, and the paucity of recruits to be obtained by him needs no further comment. Notwithstanding this great disparity in men and material, it can be shown that, within the four months during which Sheridan commanded the cavalry of the Army of the Potomac, Hampton was never routed in a single engagement, and generally achieved substantial successes. The same assertion is equally true of that period of the campaign of 1864 subsequent to August 2d, at which date Sheridan was transferred to command in the Shenandoah Valley. With the advent of Hampton to the control of the cavalry of the Army of Northern Virginia came a great change in tactics. Before this time the practice had been to operate cavalry mounted, the dismounted men, or sharp-shooters, being generally merely auxiliary to the mounted men, covering their flanks when needed. Much brilliant manouvering had been done, many enterprising raids executed, and some very good service performed in confusing the enemy and obtaining an insight into his plans. But the time had arrived when a change in system was necessary The Federal cavalry, thanks to Pleasanton, were better organized and equipped and stronger in numbers than ever before. A new man was now at their head, who was bent upon obtaining promotion. Sheridan's experiences in the West had been almost entirely as an infantry officer, and he was disposed to fight his cavalry harder than his predecessor had done. This of itself would have brought about a change. The nature of most of the country campaigned in made mounted charges by the Confederates on a large scale against reliable troops armed with magazine rifles usually impossible or suicidal. But, besides this, there were other reasons for the change. Hampton was born a soldier. He grasped the situation confronting him. The only way in which his men, relatively few in numbers and badly equipped, could be made to check Sheridan was by abler handling and harder fighting as well as finer strategy. In dismounted fighting, performed skirmish-style in cover, where practicable, in a thin line to be strengthened, when advisable, the muzzle-loaders and smaller numbers were not at such a great disadvantage, for man to man his troopers were very much better shots than their adversaries. He could dash his force, mounted, to favorable points with great celerity, dismount and rush them in, and, if advisable, draw them out as quickly and hurl them fiercely on some other and weaker position. Thus he virtually multiplied his men, and the enemy would form an exaggerated impression of his numbers, and frequently mistook his cavalry for their *bete noir*—reinforcements of infantry. And all this did not militate in the least against the efficiency of his command as a mounted force to be thus used, and brilliantly used, too, when occasion offered. We maintain that Hampton succeeded in making his men good, hard-fighting infantry on occasion, capable of practically doubling or quadrupling their strength by celerity of movement, and at the same time preserved intact all their good qualities as cavalry ; and we contend that no man ever before had done this on the same scale so thoroughly. In saying this, there is no intention of belittling the military genius of Forrest, which is undeniable. Only two cavalry officers in the Confederate army attained the commission of Lieutenant-Generals. These were Hampton and Forrest—ranking in the order named. Wheeler is frequently referred to in newspapers as a Lieutenant-General, and Appleton's Cyclopædia of American Biography states that he was so, but this is a mistake: he was a Major-General.

The battles of Spotsylvania had now been fought and won by Lee. Grant was compelled, therefore, to make fresh endeavors elsewhere to turn the Confederate flank. The cavalry were thus kept busy, the Federals in trying to mask the movements of their infantry, Hampton in tearing away the mask and in concealing the dispositions taking place in his own army.

Cavalry fighting went on daily it is only some of the affairs which we notice here. On May 15th Rosser had made a daring and successful reconnoissance in the direction of Fredericksburg, driving in all the cavalry he met and developing the position of Grant's right flank. On May 19th Hampton was again engaged, co-operating in a movement made by General Ewell, and did effective service. Also on May 21st, there was fighting in connection with Grant's movement on Hanover Junction, and this continued in a desultory way until he moved off. Hampton then marched to Atlee's station, where he received orders from Lee to ascertain if the Federal infantry had crossed to the south of the Pamunkey river

Sheridan, after his Richmond raid, had rested

and recruited his force, and on May 25th reached Chesterfield station, on the North Anna river, there reporting back to Grant's army. On the following day a further movement to the left was made by the Federal army, Sheridan with the First and Second divisions of his corps leading. His Third division was detached to the right flank. Sheridan crossed to the south bank of the Pamunkey river on May 27th, and the infantry followed on the next day.

It was of vital importance to discover whether or not the Federal infantry in force had crossed, or were crossing, the river. To ascertain this promptly was necessary at any expense. To do this it was indispensable to drive back Sheridan's cavalry to such an extent at least as to reveal the real position of his infantry. If the latter had not crossed the river, dispositions would have to be made by Lee to confront him farther to his left.

In pursuance of the orders above mentioned

as received from Lee, Hampton moved out on the morning of May 28th with W H. F Lee's division, and Wickham's brigade of Fitz Lee's division, and Rosser's brigade, and the Fourth and part of the Fifth South Carolina regiments of Butler's brigade. It happened that Sheridan was also in motion for the purpose of trying to find out the position of the Confederate infantry.

The engagement which took place, and lasted from about 10 A. M. until 5 P M., has been called by both Hampton and Sheridan the most severe cavalry fighting of the war, and is designated by the name of Hawes' Shop, which was near where the collision occurred. The reader has very likely never even heard the name of this " cavalry affair," and will have forgotten it within ten minutes. Such is the fame of the cavalry !

Only about half of the Fourth South Carolina was present that day, the rest being detained in camp, as their horses were temporarily disabled by sore backs. All but one hundred men of the Fifth South Carolina were there. The Sixth South Carolina did not report until the following night. These regiments, newly arrived in Virginia, were well organized and disciplined, but had hitherto seen but little service. Some of the newest recruits had never yet heard the "zip" of a bullet. As they marched along the roads there would be, from time to time, partial blocks and stoppages to allow wagon-trains and troops to pass, as the infantry were moving to new positions. Then these boys looked for the first time upon the columns of the Army of Northern Virginia marshalling for battle, and a grand sight it was. There were no bands of music nor gorgeous uniforms ; none of the artificial "frills" of war. There was no need of these, for here, magnificent in simplicity, ragged, battle-stained, and gaunt, but confident and cheery, marched the victors of the Wilderness and Spotsylvania.

So the Greek athlete was most beautiful when chest was bared and limbs stripped for conflict. The intervals between parts of the cavalry column, caused by the interruptions mentioned, would be closed up on a canter when the obstructions were removed. As the place where the fighting had already commenced was approached, within sound of the rattle of small arms and the boom of artillery, they had space for a gallop, and soon reached the fringe of the fire. Ah! how their hearts beat and blood coursed, and the horses, forgetting fatigue, seemed equally excited. All these sights and sounds, entirely new experiences, appeared to be strangely familiar, probably because of the hereditary memories of a warlike race. "Dismount to fight!" Nos. 1, 2, and 3 dismount and attach together their horses by the bridle-reins, and No. 4, mounted, must lead them, sheltered from shots. Many of the horses were well-bred pets from home. Aroused by the gallop, thinking, perhaps, a hunt was on foot, they are now disappointed, worried, and uneasy. So their big, soft eyes look troubled, and they whinny and neigh, and stretch forward their heads for caresses. Then they sidle up into orderly ranks and patiently await the return of masters who, perhaps, never come back again.

When Hampton encountered Sheridan's advance-guard, he drove it in upon the main body, which he then vigorously attacked with Wickham's and Rosser's brigades, and soon the two regiments of Butler's brigade were put in on Wickham's right. Thus Rosser was on the left, Wickham in the centre, and Butler's two regiments on the right, the Fourth South Carolina occupying the extreme right. W H. F Lee's division was sent by a road leading to the left in the hope of turning the Federal right flank, but this proved impracticable, and he could only use the artillery and cover Rosser's left.

The Federals were at first pressed back, having only their Second division, General Gregg commanding, engaged, but being reinforced from the First division they held their ground. It was discovered also from infantry prisoners that the Federal infantry in force were just behind their cavalry on the south bank of the Pamunkey river, in supporting distance. It was evidently, therefore, useless to pursue the fight further, the object of the reconnoissance being gained on obtaining this information.

The order was consequently given to withdraw from in front of the combined cavalry and infantry. This was effected without difficulty by Rosser, and in excellent style. Wickham's brigade was also got out promptly But the two regiments of Butler's brigade did not fare so well. General Butler had not yet returned from an absence caused by a severe wound, and the regimental officers, as well as the men, had had no experience in this sort of warfare. The engagement took place in a thick wood with much dense undercover. This was an advantage to the Confederates, who availed themselves of the trees and logs and inequalities in the ground for protection, and could thus obtain the benefit of their greater skill in shooting. They were doing good execution from their long rifles with the terrible Minies, and had no idea they were intended to leave their position. Moreover, the denseness of the cover, together with the smoke, much increased the difficulty of passing along the line the order to fall back. So it happened that these regiments became flanked and suffered considerably. General Hampton, perceiving that something was wrong, rode in and brought them out in good order, and formed them two or three hundred yards back across an open field, where a thrown-down fence afforded some protection. Here they awaited "their friends the enemy," but the latter had had enough and did not advance. The presence of Hampton, calm, cool, and reassuring, had braced up every one. The men never doubted it was "all right" when he told them so. And his kind words to them that night just before dismounting at camp, and his concern for their casualties, dwelt in their memories ever afterwards.

There was a squadron of the Fourth South Carolina on the extreme right which suffered more than the others. Couriers sent to order them out were killed, and consequently they received no instructions to fall back, and being separated by thick cover from the rest, remained, continuing to fight on as before. At length the right company (Company K, Charleston Light Dragoons) was surrounded on three sides, perceiving which, Lieutenant Nowell, in command, gave the order to retreat. This they did coolly, fighting their way through at close quarters in good order, and successfully took position in good shape on the right of their re-formed regimental line. Out of forty-seven dismounted men taken in, they lost nineteen and an officer, and only one unwounded prisoner, a youth only eighteen years of age. As, however, they were very good shots with both rifle and pistol, and did not fire in wild volleys, but singly and coolly in sportsmanlike style, it is not at all unlikely the company inflicted three casualties for every one received. The spirit existing among them may be judged by the following incident: One of their number had been shot through the arm, and obliged, therefore, to drop his rifle, but he had come out with the others, holding his pistol in the sound hand. Some one offered to relieve him of the pistol, but he declined, saying,

"I want that to shoot a surgeon,"

and all who heard the remark, laughed. As a matter of fact he retained the pistol in the hospital, and his arm, too. Poor boys! No one ever fought better, but their ranks suffered heavily, far more heavily than any other company engaged. But not far wrong were our Pagan ancestors, who believed that the souls of those who bravely fell in honorable battle were transported at once, all sins forgiven, to Valhalla. Surely the Christian's God could do no less.

The character of the fighting done in this engagement may, perhaps, be best judged by the impression it produced on the Federals who witnessed it. General Custer refers to Butler's brigade, which took into the fight less than one thousand dismounted men, as consisting "of seven large regiments, principally from South Carolina," and says of his own brigade: "Our loss was greater than in any other engagement of the campaign. We held our position until after dark, when we were relieved by the infantry." Colonel Kester, First New Jersey Cavalry, reports to the Governor of

An improvised hospital. This was a barn turned hurriedly into a receiving station for wounded men.

his State that the battle was "the severest cavalry fighting of the war. The enemy was a new brigade from South Carolina, and was very formidable." Alger, Fifth Michigan Cavalry, says it was "an obstinate resistance, fighting our men hand to hand." General Davies, in his "Life of Sheridan," writes: "Much of the very stubborn resistance exhibited in this action was due to the presence in the field of the troops from South Carolina referred to. This brigade, raised in South Carolina at the beginning of the war, had never before left that State, nor had seen any active service, and when, with full ranks, and weapons and uniforms all fresh and untarnished by war or service, they joined the veterans who had been for three years exposed to the losses and trials of active duty in the field, their reception was not of the warmest, and it was not thought that much could be expected from them. The existence of this prejudice, and their own desire to show themselves at least the equals of their comrades, caused them to exhibit a desperate courage in this, their first engagement, and, as was said by veterans on both sides, they were too inexperienced to know when they had suffered defeat, and continued to resist long after it was apparent that the position they held was turned and efforts to maintain it were hopeless." A staff officer of Sheridan's has stated, to the writer's personal knowledge, that his General was very much worried over the losses his command had sustained in this action, which he said were the heaviest he had ever suffered in proportion to the number engaged. He remarked, "It is the first time we have met those Carolinians of Butler's, and I wish to God it might be the last." In his official report he says that the Confederate force "appeared to be the cavalry corps and a brigade of South Carolina troops reported 4,000 strong and armed with long-range rifles, commanded by a Colonel Butler: these Carolinians fought very gallantly in this their first fight, judging from the number of their dead and wounded and prisoners captured." It should be remembered that that the fighting on the part of the Confederates was done by two brigades and two regiments of South Carolina troops, the latter numbering less than 1,000 instead of 4,000, as stated. He speaks of it as an "unequal contest," and so it was, but in a sense opposite to that intended by him. He also adds that the battle "was fought almost immediately in front of the infantry line of our army, which was busily occupied throwing up breastworks." This accounts for the fact that infantry prisoners were captured by Hampton, and would seem to prove that they must have been engaged.

These, among many similar quotations which might be given, sufficiently illustrate what was thought of Butler's "long-shooters." The implication of "defeat" is absolutely unfounded, the withdrawal being made as a matter of course, after the enemy's position was developed and the fact was established that the brigades of Rosser, Wickham, and two regiments of Butler were attacking the combined cavalry and infantry of the Army of the Potomac.

This reconnoissance, made in pursuance of orders from Lee, was perfectly successful in its chief and all-important object—ascertaining clearly the position of the Federal infantry. It was one of the steps in the manœuvres of Lee leading up to Cold Harbor, and, as that battle was a decisive victory for the Confederates, the preliminaries must have been successfully managed by Hampton both in demonstrating the movements of the Federal infantry and in veiling those of his own army. Perhaps if Sheridan, possessing such an immense superiority in numbers and equipment, had refrained from the fruitless excursion to Richmond and confined his efforts more closely to the normal functions of the cavalry of a great army, the battles of the Wilderness and Spotsylvania might have had different results for his friends. It is said by one writer that his Richmond raid came about from its being reported to General Grant by Meade that Sheridan had said he "could beat Hampton's cavalry" if permitted to act independently, upon which General Grant replied:

"Does he say that? Then let him go and do it."

He went, but did not "do it," and meantime left his army groping in the dark.

The engagement at Hawes' Shop gave a serious experience to the Federal cavalry, one which they never forgot, and they courted no renewals of similar contests. It also increased the prestige of Hampton's cavalry with the infantry of their own army, and many kindly greetings came from these veterans to the newcomers during the following few days.

The Federal losses must have been heavy, for some days afterwards, in passing the house where their hospital had been established, General Hampton was informed that one thousand and four of their wounded had been brought there.

While the fight was going on, Hampton sent a note to General Early, who was then stationed at Pole Green church, suggesting to him to move down in the direction of Old Church, and then by turning to his left to gain the rear of the force opposed to Hampton. General Early did not concur in the advisability of this movement, which subsequent information showed to have been practicable, and from which, it is thought, important results would have been obtained.

Brigadier-General M. C. Butler reported for duty on the night of May 28th, and took command of his own brigade, the Fourth, Fifth, and Sixth South Carolina, which was then ordered to Meadow bridge for the purpose of being organized. This object, however, was not attained There was so much smell of saltpetre in the air in those days that a fight always came about easily. On May 30th Butler with his brigade and a part of Gary's attacked, at Matadequin creek, a force which proved to be the extreme left of the Federal army. The Federals were posted behind a farm-house and some out-buildings, a rail fence extending on each side. The attack was made across an open wheat field, and then from cover of a thrown-down fence on a road on the farther side of the field. The enemy made a stout resistance, but were driven from their position. But there was an unpleasant sequel. Reinforcements came to them. To the left of the Confederates, down the road they were holding, marched in close order, covering it from side to side, a dense mass of blue. The long-range Enfields fired at will into that mass could not fail to do their work, but the satisfaction of practicing at a large target is marred when the component atoms are shooting back, especially as the slender cover of fence-rails, seeming preternaturally thin, was enfiladed as soon as this mass of blue deployed. So Butler's force was compelled to leave, nor stand upon the order of their going, as the field behind was entirely open and the bullets were industriously mowing down the wheat. It was a plucky fight, but to have been successful it would have been necessary to beat the left wing of Grant's army, a feat which would have eclipsed David's exploit against Goliath. This engagement is sometimes designated as Cold Harbor, but is more properly called Matadequin Creek.

After the Hawes' Shop engagement the Confederate cavalry continued to confront the enemy, Fitz. Lee's division being stationed on the right, W H. F Lee's division on the left, and Hampton with Rosser's and Young's brigades near Atlee's station. On May 31st W H. F Lee had a sharp skirmish at Hanover Courthouse, and the next morning was attacked by Wilson's division and fell back in the direction of Ashland. Hampton moved to his assistance with three regiments of Rosser's brigade, and struck Wison's column, throwing it into great confusion. Rosser followed up the advantage by a series of brilliant mounted charges, some of them over dismounted men, and drove Wilson into Ashland with the sabre, capturing prisoners from eight different regiments, about two hundred horses, and many arms. Wilson made a stand in Ashland, posting his artillery in the village, and his men behind the houses and the railway embankment. The North Carolina brigade of W H. F Lee's division was then dismounted and charged the enemy, but did not at first succeed in dislodging him, Brigadier-General Young, temporarily in command of the brigade, being wounded. At this juncture Hampton, taking with him a regiment and two squadrons, gallantly dashed in on Wilson's right flank and gave him the *coup de grace*. After that, it was simply a pursuit until night compelled the victors to halt. Many prisoners were captured, and Wilson sent in a flag of truce for his wounded.

General Hampton received the congratulations of Lee for his success Lee also expressed his "gratification at the handsome conduct of Rosser's command and his thanks for their having so gallantly defeated the enemy."

On June 3d Hampton made a reconnoissance with W H. F Lee's division towards Hawes' Shop, the scene of the engagement of May 28th, and found the Federals posted in earth-works near the shop. The North Carolina brigade, Colonel Baker commanding, was then dismounted, and, after a sharp affair, carried the works in handsome style, driving the enemy to an interior line.

On June 3d also occurred a much more memorable event, the battle of Cold Harbor. On that morning, Grant's army there present, nearly 113,000 troops, gallantly flung themselves upon Lee's columns and were repulsed with the slaughter of 13,000 men in an incredibly short space of time, about one hour. The successive advances and recoils could be numbered by a listener at a distance from the awful roar of musketry and artillery, and then the comparative cessation for short intervals. At length the Federal soldiers sullenly refused to obey orders to advance again to meet in their ranks the fruitless butchery of twenty to every one Confederate disabled. And thus was ended Grant's "Overland Campaign." Another move to the left, endeavoring to turn Lee's flank, would put him further from, not nearer to the objective, Richmond. So he began to fortify his position confronting Lee, but soon abandoned the idea of a siege and commenced on June 12th to move his army to the south of the James river, there to sit down for ten weary months before Petersburg. Thus he had changed his mind, and would *not* "fight it out on that line, if it took all summer," Lee's logic having proved convincing.

The following quotations are from "The Army of the Potomac," by the Federal historian Swinton, who is writing about an army for which he had the greatest admiration and love:

> "It took hardly more than ten minutes of the figment men call time to decide the battle. There was along the whole line a rush, the spectacle of impregnable works, a bloody loss, then a sullen falling back and the action was decided.
>
> * * * * * *
>
> "The action was decided, as I have said, in an incredibly brief time in the morning s

assault. But rapidly as the result was reached it was decisive, for the consciousness of every man pronounced further assault hopeless. The troops went forward as far as the example of their officers could carry them, nor was it possible to urge them beyond, for there they knew lay only death, without even the chance of victory.

*   *   *   *   *   *

"Grant's loss in the series of actions from the Wilderness to the Chickahominy reached the enormous aggregate of sixty thousand men put *hors de combat*, a number greater than the entire strength of Lee's army at the opening of the campaign. He had inflicted on Lee a loss of twenty thousand, the ratio being one to three. The Confederates, elated at the skillful manner in which they had constantly been thrust between Richmond and the Union army, and conscious of the terrible price in blood they had exacted from the latter, were in high spirit, and the *morale* of Lee's army was never better than after the battle of Cold Harbor.

*   *   *   *   *   *

"The result of such assaults as that of Spotsylvania Courthouse and at Cold Harbor, in the latter of which the Army of the Potomac lost at least twenty men to Lee's one, presents the *reductio ad absurdum* of the theory of hammering.

*   *   *   *   *   *

"Now, so gloomy was the military outlook after the action on the Chickahominy, and to such a degree, by consequence, had the moral spring of the public mind become relaxed, that there was at this time great danger of a collapse of the war. The history of this conflict truthfully written will show this. Had not success elsewhere come to brighten the horizon, it would have been difficult to raise new forces to recruit the Army of the Potomac, which, shaken in its structure, its valor quenched in blood, and thou-

Capturing a Federal wagon train. Uncle Sam aiding the Confederate Quartermaster's Department.

sands of its ablest officers killed and wounded, was the Army of the Potomac no more."

Probably no impartial critic will now deny that the Army of the Potomac did good fighting from the Wilderness to Cold Harbor, where was met absolute defeat, rendering necessary the abandonment of the campaign on the north side of the James river against Richmond. It is likely, too, that few well-informed men doubt that at this period the question of making peace or continuing the war was trembling in the balance. But this is not all. Since Swinton, a careful student of the events of the war, wrote in 1866, there are sources of information open to all which were not accessible to him at that time, and which throw a flood of light upon much hitherto dark and unexplorable ground. We can now clearly perceive that not only were Swinton's views, which I have quoted, correct, but that, more than this, the Army of the Potomac, like a man only partially recovered from well-nigh mortal illness with a broken constitution, never again exhibited the admirable vigor exerted before Cold Harbor, and notwithstanding all the fresh blood infused into it through new recruits during the remainder of the year, was, to use a familiar expression, "under hack" to the end. But, besides this, not only was the question of war or peace in doubt during the early summer of 1864, but it was thus, too, during the entire campaign. If Lee was fighting for his life at Petersburg, so was Grant, and in a much broader sense, and well he knew it. Above him was the sword suspended by the thread which "attrition" at any moment might cut. Although the withdrawal of Lee from Richmond to better positions further inland, thus shortening and simplifying the Confederate lines of communication, and lengthening and complicating those of their enemy, and depriving the latter of his advantages by water, would have been not without political difficulties, yet it was nevertheless perfectly practicable, and we now know that this course was approved of by Lee, though not by Davis. But with Grant it was very different. His side, in the listless silence of discouragement, witnessed the abandonment of the attack on Richmond from the north side of the James, but their despair would have demanded hearing in loud and imperative voice if the siege of Petersburg had been raised. If anyone will carefully read the "Records of the Union and Confederate Armies," published under the auspices of the War Department, I think he will come to the above conclusion. Those "Records" constitute in some respects the most wonderful history ever compiled. The official reports often merely convey the impressions about events intended to be given for reasons of their own by the writers, and official tables of numbers and losses are very fallible. But this is not true of all telegrams hastily penned in the flush of excitement, amidst the sound of the tramp of marching columns, or of despatches or letters hurried off by couriers galloping through the smoke of battle, or communications written under stress and pressure, not expected to be published. These will usually contain the real thoughts and feelings, hopes and fears of the writers. There is then no time for preparation intended to deceive, and generally no desire to mislead, but an inclination to state the truth, the unvarnished truth. Such correspondence is not dramatic, it is human; not realistic, real. You seem to be hearing, not reading the words, to see the expression of the faces, to watch the anxious working of the mouth, the glance of the eyes, the twitch of the hands betraying overstrained tension of the nerves of the strong man. As you look one face flushes, another pales with suppressed excitement (and the latter is generally the better man). These living "Records" are to the mind what the Roentgen-rays are in physics. You see through and through your man—the working of the brain, the pulsation of the heart, stand revealed in light. Sometimes through many despatches he may escape you, may succeed in keeping on his mask; but watch him closely and patiently, and at length he will give himself away, divulge his secret. It may be by only a phrase, a chance expression, or even by a single word, but it will be enough to speak volumes of authentic history to light up some places hitherto veiled from you. General Meade's interior, and that of many others, is often plain to view under this mental Roentgen-ray, but even Grant, habitually cool and silent, is sometimes lighted up by a vivid if rare flash.

The cavalry engagements preceding Cold Harbor were not isolated fights, but the smaller links in the chain of scientific manœuvres leading up gradually to this crowning event. They were minor parts of a grand and symmetrical whole. To understand them thoroughly in this sense, it is necessary also to comprehend the entire defensive strategy used by Lee to defeat his antagonist. An explanation on such extended lines would far exceed the limits of this sketch and probably also the patience of the reader, but without it the military ability of Hampton cannot be fully appreciated.

CHAPTER V

THE TREVILIAN CAMPAIGN.

ON June 8th, General Hampton, with his division, was at Atlee's station, Fitz. Lee's division being at Cold Harbor Early that morning his scouts reported to Hampton that a large force of cavalry and artillery had crossed the Pamunkey river, and was moving north. This information he at once transmitted by signal to General Lee, and by letter also, suggesting in the latter that Sheridan's object was to strike at Gordonsville and Charlottesville, to destroy the railroads, and then to unite with Hunter, who was moving on Lynchburg. Supposing this to be Sheridan's object, he urged that he be allowed to pursue him, and, after a full consultation, General Lee directed him to carry out this plan.

Preparations were made accordingly, three days' rations cooked by the men, and with horse-corn fastened to their saddles, the First division marched by daylight on June 9th. The Second division, Fitz. Lee's, was ordered to follow. The Third divison, W H. F Lee's, remained with the army.

The Trevilian campaign is of special interest, because it concerned exclusively the cavalry, no infantry participating or being in possible supporting distance, either in a physical or a strategical sense. It was, pure and simple, a cavalry duel, which put to the test the relative military ability and fighting power of the antagonists. It thus possesses a picturesque, romantic charm derived from the isolation of the combatants as they wrestled for mastery, far separated from their armies, as if they had sought out this solitude to settle, uninterrupted, their quarrel by wager of battle.

The force under Hampton did not exceed 4,700 men in all in the two divisions. These figures are taken from memoranda of General Hampton, based on papers in his possession preserved from the war, and correspond with data obtained from other sources. There were three batteries of horse artillery of four guns each.

Sheridan had his First and Second divisions, commanded by Torbert and Gregg, numbering about 9,000 men, with twenty-four pieces of artillery, being six batteries of four guns each. The information about his numbers is obtained from the official returns for June 1st, as well as from captured field returns of some of his brigades. The returns of his cavalry seem not to have been regularly made during the active part of the campaign, when fighting was going on nearly every day.

The twenty-four regiments composing Sheridan's two divisions selected for this expedition consisted of the picked troops of his corps, such as the First, Second, and Fifth United States (regulars), Custer's brigade, and First New Jersey.

The Federal troops, therefore, outnumbered Hampton's in the proportion of more than two to one, with artillery in the same ratio. But this was not all. Their armament and equipment, their breech-loaders and magazine rifles, gave them an advantage over muzzle-loaders, which ought to have been the equivalent of a hundred per cent., but estimating it at only fifty per cent., their force would have practically outnumbered Hampton's as three is to one.

On the morning of June 8th Sheridan slipped quietly out of the back door of his army, crossed the Pamunkey river at Newcastle, took a northerly course for about ten miles, and then turning a little to the north of west, proceeded nearly parallel with the north bank of the North Anna river, a branch of the Pamunkey

Hampton had read his purpose aright. Sheridan had received orders to march upon Charlottesville and Gordonsville, destroying everything there of value to the army, and he was to tear up and so effectually ruin the Virginia Central railroad (now the Chesapeake and Ohio) as to cut off supplies from the Shenandoah Valley, which were essential to the subsistence of Lee's army. After that he was to form a junction with General Hunter, who had been operating in the Valley, and in connection with him, capture Lynchburg, burn the stores there, and then return with him to the Army of the Potomac, destroying *en route* the James River canal, with discretion to work any other mischief he could do. How entirely he failed to accomplish these purposes, or any one of them, or anything else of value to Grant, the facts will show.

Sheridan's march for the first three days was only a hot, dusty summer ride, for passing out through the rear of his army he traversed a region where only women and children or weakly non-combative men were to be found. On the evening of the third day he crossed the North Anna river at Carpenter's ford, about sixty-five miles from his starting point, camping near there on the road leading to Trevilian station, a few miles distant. Torbert's division was in advance, and when it was going into camp ten or twelve men dashed at the head of the column, fired their pistols and galloped off. These were, in fact, Hampton's scouts, but Torbert supposed them to be merely some countrymen, home-guards; and this was the only intimation detected by him of an enemy being at hand, as he himself says, and the evidence of others corroborates this. So Sheridan and his nine thousand followers peacefully bivouacked under the summer stars, sup posing the Confederate cavalry to be many miles away.

But Hampton had been up and doing. Starting on the morning of June 9th, one day behind Sheridan, he took a shorter route and made all speed to place his command between his antagonist and the latter's objective point. The weather was hot, and an unusually severe drought was prevailing. The dust raised by the marching columns was stifling, and the only water obtainable for man or beast was from small streams crossed, and this, churned up by thousands of hoofs, was almost undrinkable. By the night of June 10th Hampton's division reached Green Spring Valley, three miles from Trevilian station, on the (then styled) Virginia Central railroad, and there went into camp. At nearly the same time Fitzhugh Lee's division reached Louisa Courthouse, about five miles from Trevilian, also on the railroad, near which they halted for the night. By this time it was pretty well known among the men that Hampton was seeking Sheridan, and that a fight was on for the morning. During the first day of the march not only the troopers, but even the brigade commanders were ignorant of the object of the expedition and where they were going, and many believed a dash on Washington was intended. It was somewhat a disappointment to give up that prospect, but soon the weary riders and horses were stretched on the ground asleep, both equally careless of what the morrow would bring forth.

By daylight the next morning, quietly, without blast of bugle or other needless sound, all the command was in ranks in readiness to advance to the attack. The air was crisp and bracing and sweet with the smell of clover, and the foot-hills of the Blue Ridge looked cool and refreshing after all the dust and heat of the previous day. From the Federal camps floated the strains of the bugle sounding reveille.

Hampton's plan of battle was as follows: From Trevilian's station, near which his division then was, a road ran in a northerly direction to Carpenter's ford, on the North Anna river, and on this road was Sheridan. Another road led from Louisa Courthouse, where Fitz. Lee's division had camped, towards Carpenter's ford, joining the Trevilian road at Clayton's store. Fitz. Lee was ordered to move down this road towards Clayton's store and engage the enemy when met, and Hampton's division proceeded to the attack down the Trevilian road towards Clayton's store, except Rosser's brigade, which took position covering a road to the left, leading to Gordonsville. By this programme, if properly carried out, Hampton's division's right flank would cover Fitz. Lee's left, drawing the enemy back towards Clayton's store, where the two divisions would form a junction, and thus strike Sheridan on flank as well as front. Hemmed in and crowded together, with a river in the rear, he could then be destroyed. This was no visionary scheme, nor wild, foolhardy attempt to accomplish what was impracticable, or involved too great risk, but was a deliberately and wisely-laid plan for virtually annihilating the cavalry of the Army of the Potomac. The ground was well chosen for the purpose, and the nature of the country along the Trevilian road lent itself admirably to the design. It was thickly wooded, and would thus conceal numbers and disposition, and afford the men the advantage of their superior skill as shots, and in this way neutralize to a certain extent the greater effectiveness of the enemy's magazine rifles. It is a little amusing that Federal officers on this and on other occasions complained of Hampton as a " woods fighter," as if such tactics were hardly fair play. That they did so, however, is, in fact, a compliment, and gives evidence of the gift he possessed of detecting at a glance advantages of ground and utilizing favorable positions. So was La Roche Jacquelin a "woods fighter" when the forests of La Vendee rang with musketry and proved grave-yards for the armies of "*liberte, egalite, fraternite.*"

According to the plan Hampton's division marched forward to the attack, and Fitz. Lee reported his force moving out in obedience to orders. A squadron of the Fourth South Carolina went in advance, and had not proceeded far down the road before they were yelling and charging and driving in the enemy's picket or advance guard. Then Butler's and Young's brigades, of Hampton's division, were dismounted, and advancing through the woods on each side of the road soon struck the enemy and pressed him back, according to the plan. It seems from the reports of the Federal generals that they were still in the dark as to the nature of the force opposing them, and from the character of the ground could form no estimate of the numbers. Custer was, consequently, ordered to take his brigade to Trevilian station and there form a junction with the rest of Torbert's division—the General being under the impression that he was encountering only some raw country militia which he could drive before him. In trying to execute this movement Custer met the left of Fitz. Lee's division, and there was some little skirmishing, but it was so feebly conducted by the Confederate brigade engaged that Custer drew off down a by-road, which he had discovered, leading to Trevilian station, and thus passed between the two divisions, placing himself in the rear of Hampton's. This could not have happened if Fitz. Lee's division had advanced in the manner ordered. This it is necessary to comprehend clearly, for the failure to succeed in the plan of battle originally conceived was due only to this. The plan of battle was thus frustrated. Word was brought to Hampton that the enemy was in his rear, and he galloped to the spot to find it too true. In this emergency orders were sent to Rosser to attack Custer, and promptly a clatter of hoofs and cloud of dust announced him coming at the head of the "Laurel brigade," and soon the crack of pistols and the swish of sabres made sad work in Custer's ranks. The led horses of Butler's brigade, three caissons, and wagons, which Custer had captured, were all retaken and retained; nearly an entire regiment was made prisoners, and four caissons and the headquarter wagon of Custer, with brigade reports and private correspondence, were run into Fitz. Lee, who picked them up and kept them. Unfortunately the gallant Rosser was wounded in the charge. Meantime the tide had turned against Butler's and Young's brigades, for the enemy had availed himself of the opportunity afforded by the separation of their flank from

Fitz. Lee's division, to come through the gap round the right flank of Hampton's division, thus compelling it to fall back. The situation was very grave; indeed, in view of the original disparity of numbers and the present position of his command, it might well have been that Hampton should have utterly despaired of success, and only hoped at best to save a part of his troops by a hasty retreat. But nothing was farther from his mind than such thoughts. He dashed about, personally giving orders and despatching staff-officers and couriers, steadying and encouraging every one by his own splendid gallantry. His purpose to beat Sheridan remained unalterably fixed, and he inspired confidence that he would do it. At this critical, well-nigh desperate juncture, as it appeared to most present, he displayed the highest qualities of a commander, and literally plucked victory out of the jaws of defeat.

This was the situation. Hampton's division

was flanked, nearly surrounded and compelled to fall back. Fitz. Lee's division was pushed to the east towards Louisa Courthouse and isolated, becoming thus of no use until the afternoon of the following day. The whole of Sheridan's force was consequently available to crush the life out of Hampton's division and could then have dealt at leisure with Fitz. Lee's; only superior generalship foiled this.

Hampton kept up the fighting, but gradually withdrew his men to the west, a short distance from Trevilian station, until he reached a naturally strong position, and there established a new line along the railroad embankment and road leading to Gordonsville, thus covering that place and Charlottesville. Here he was assailed by Sheridan, but without success, and night closed in and morning came with the positions unchanged. At about midday Fitz. Lee reported, having succeeded by a detour round the enemy in reaching the rest of the command. It was after three o'clock when at length Sheridan again attacked. He had no alternative but this or retreat and failure, for Hampton covered Gordonsville and Charlottesville and the Virginia Central railroad, the objective points of his expedition. Fitz. Lee was ordered to strengthen the left of Butler's brigade with one of his brigades, and with the other to make a circuit to the left and strike the enemy on his right flank.

Hampton's line was protected in part by the railroad embankment, but stretched along the intersecting wagon-road leading to Gordonsville, which gave it somewhat the shape of a flattened V. On this part of the line there were no rifle-pits, the only cover consisting of such few fence-rails as could be obtained and a little earth hastily thrown up by the help of tin plates and cups, or, if need be, scooped up with the hands. These improvised defences (which the reports of the Federal generals have styled "fortifications" and "rifle-pits") were a quite inadequate protection against bullets, and afforded no relief at all from artillery It was along this road that most of M. C. Butler's brigade was posted. Butler, this day commanding Hampton's division, was soon to gain the well-earned commission of a major-general. Always calm and cool when in action, his handsome, clear-cut face showed on this occasion no emotion as he scanned the details of the field.

The Federals evidently quite realized that on the issue of the fight commencing depended the success or failure of their expedition. Nothing of importance had been accomplished by them thus far, for they had torn up only a hundred feet or so of railroad track at Trevilian station, which could be restored easily without any interruption of consequence to the road. They therefore attacked with great spirit, coming up handsomely within short pistol-shot of the Confederate line, keeping up a continuous fire from their magazine rifles during the charges, but each time met the steady shots of the muzzle-loaders fired "at will" by expert hands, and each time recoiled, leaving their dead and wounded on the field. Meantime in artillery they had a great advantage and used it well. Major Chew, commanding Hampton's batteries, fought his guns with indomitable pluck and great skill, and Hart's pieces did splendid work, but they were overmatched in the proportion of two against one. Butler's unprotected line along the Gordonsville road was compelled to bear the brunt of the fire. Here at one time cartridges became exhausted, and while waiting for replenishment the men had to endure shell and grape without the comfort of hitting back, a hard thing to do. What made it worse was, that some of the poor fellows said they could see the Federals serving out to their troopers drams of whiskey, which was very tantalizing under the circumstances, it must be confessed, even by teetotalers. At length an ammunition-wagon came clattering along just behind the line, the horses at full gallop, the driver loudly cracking his whip and a man in the rear frantically throwing out packages of cartridges, which were eagerly caught up, as hungry dogs seize food thrown to them.

<u>Seven charges in all were made.</u> When the last was in progress the flashes of the rifles of Fitz. Lee announced that he had accomplished his mission and was on the enemy's flank. Just then a Federal caisson was blown up by a Confederate shell, doing considerable damage. At that moment, as if this explosion had been a signal prearranged, the whole of Hampton's line sprang to their feet, leaped over the breastwork and down the embankment, and with a wild yell charged, sweeping the enemy back in rapid retreat. That ended the matter, the Federals after this only keeping up some irregular firing

to cover their rearward movement. By this time it was ten o'clock at night. Sheridan's entire column, leaving dead and wounded on the field, moved rapidly down the road towards Carpenter's ford, and continued without halt all night, retreating by the same route by which it had come. Orders were at once given by General Hampton to make pursuit, and Fitz. Lee was directed to cut off the enemy from Carpenter's ford, but this he did not accomplish, and it was therefore not until about daylight that anything serious was done. Meantime Sheridan had gained a start of several hours, which enabled him to cross the river

In this affair 695 prisoners, including 125 wounded, were captured by Hampton. The losses in his division amounted to 59 killed, 258 wounded, and 295 missing, and the losses in Fitz. Lee's division were very small. The Federal reports speak of their having carried off about 500 of their wounded, and their dead

The explosion of the caisson, which seemed to give the signal for the victorious charge at Trevilian's, Louisa County, Va., June 12, 1864.

and badly wounded left behind were numerous, owing to the very severe effect produced by the Minie bullets used in the muzzle-loaders. As soon as practicable the Confederate wounded, and such of the Federals as were in a condition to be moved, were brought down to the railroad and shipped to the hospital at Gordonsville. Some construction cars, without springs and open to the weather, were used, a rough mode of transportation, but the best that could be found. While awaiting the arrival of the train, women from the neighborhood collected, bringing for the wounded what little food they could find. It was little enough, but it was all they had, for their stores had been consumed or plundered by the Federals, and destroyed in wanton mischief in many cases. All this, however, made no difference to them. They first attended to the wants of the half-starved Confederates, and then went their rounds with equal care among the wounded Federals. It was a sermon as effective as that on the Mount—a fitting sequel, certainly; a consequence, if you like.

Official reports of battles are naturally likely to be incorrect, because they are written before the heat of conflict has subsided, and a general is tempted to make a better showing for himself than facts warrant. Misrepresentations are also often the result of false information received from others.

General Sheridan has fallen into many material errors in his report of this battle. He leaves one under the impression that the proximity of Hampton was known to him the day before the battle, but this is contradicted by the statements of Torbert, who was in the advance, and of others of his officers, which prove he was surprised. Sheridan says he commenced the fight by attacking the Confederates occupying fortifications, but in fact the Confederates were the attacking party, and had no fortifications whatever. He remarks that infantry reinforcements were received by Hampton in the second day's fight, and states that infantry were at Gordonsville, and gives this as among his reasons for not carrying out the purposes of his expedition ; but there was no infantry in the fight, and none at Gordonsville, nor nearer than Richmond. He speaks of Hampton's force holding rifle-pits, and being relieved by troops in a train of cars from Gordonsville, but there were no rifle-pits, and no train of cars, and no troops. He claims in one place to have captured only 370 prisoners, and in another 500, yet the entire list of "missing" from Hampton's division, the only division from which he could have made captures, was 295. Many of these were wounded, and some were detailed as nurses, but were carried off as prisoners. He would lead one to suppose that he destroyed the railroad between Trevilian station and Louisa Courthouse, but in fact he never reached Louisa Courthouse at all, and it was only for a hundred or two feet at Trevilian station that the railroad was interrupted, and the break there was a trifling injury easily repaired.

General Torbert says, "They have a great advantage over us from the fact that they have a very large brigade of mounted infantry armed with the rifle musket." This, of course, alluded to the muzzle-loaders of Butler's men, and to assert that these gave an advantage to troops fighting against magazine rifles, is about as reasonable as to say that bows and arrows are better weapons than fire-arms.

On the person of a Federal prisoner, captured during their retreat, was found a diary, now in the possession of General Hampton, with the following entries:

"Saturday, June 11th. Fight at Trevilian station. Captured and killed 600 rebs.

"Sunday, June 12th. Fought on same ground. Got whipped like the devil. Lost more men than the rebs did the day previous.

"Monday, June 13th. Retreat back towards Fredericksburg."

In an account of this affair written by General Davies, it is said that 500 prisoners were taken by Custer in the fight on Saturday morning, but he has certainly been misinformed. Not only was that number of prisoners not lost at all, but, besides this, Custer's brigade was in no condition to make captures, having been torn to pieces by Rosser, a fourth at least of his command placed *hors de combat*, or made prisoners, and his train, headquarter wagon, and caissons captured and carried off.

On June 14th, in a letter to General Lee, the following remark about the Trevilian fight is made by General Hampton:

"Butler's brigade held their ground against seven desperate charges under as heavy fire— artillery and musketry—as troops are often subjected to, without even giving way a foot."

Let us sum up General Sheridan's part in this

fight. He was in the dark concerning Hampton's whereabouts, was surprised by the attack, and in a dangerous position, if the orders given by Hampton had been carried out by Fitz. Lee. He seemed to be lacking in information about the topography of the country, and to be groping somewhat in the dark. Custer's demonstration in the rear of Hampton happened accidentally, but when it occured, this opportunity ought to have sufficed him to overwhelm Hampton's division by sheer weight of numbers, the odds then being three against one. By delay in renewing his attack until the afternoon of the second day, time was allowed Fitz. Lee's division, until then separated and useless, to form a junction with Hampton's division and thus to render assistance.

Sheridan having crossed the North Anna river at Carpenter's ford during the night of June 12th, proceeded to Spotsylvania Courthouse and thence across the Mattaponi and down its north bank, pursuing a not materially different route in his retreat from that taken in his advance, and reached White House, on the Pamunkey river, on June 20th. During these eight days Hampton, in following Sheridan, was compelled to keep upon the south or opposite bank of the rivers in order to interpose his force between him and Grant's army, which he was seeking to rejoin. In this way, too, the Virginia Central railroad was effectually covered from molestation. This course, instead of a direct pursuit, was rendered necessary because Sheridan was provided with a pontoon-train enabling him to cross the rivers at any point, whilst Hampton had no pontoons. The two commands, however, were near together during these eight days, frequently in sight of each other, and there were occasional small skirmishes, Hampton pressing and seeking to bring his antagonist to battle, which the latter always studiously declined.

Shortly before reaching White House, Sheridan, who had been shut off from news for eight days, received intelligence from his army, which had before this effected its retreat to the south side of the James river, and commenced the siege of Petersburg. Orders were given him to break up the depot at White House, and to convoy the supplies to his army, guarding them in transit by the infantry garrison and his two divisions of cavalry. Previous to Sheridan's reaching White House, and while he was occupied forwarding his wounded to Washington by transports on the York river, Hampton sent Fitz. Lee to capture the depot at White House. A demonstration was accordingly made and several pieces of artillery were opened upon the position, but Fitz. Lee reported it to be too strong for him. It appears that the garrison consisted of 2,444 infantry and some artillery. The capture of the stores, and depriving Sheridan of reinforcement from the troops there, would have been a good stroke. Considerable anxiety was felt at Grant's headquarters about the fate of this place, and many despatches were exchanged.

After resting for a day at White House, Sheridan, thus reinforced, commenced to march in the direction of the James river, escorting a train of 800 wagons, and managed to cross the Chickahominy. There was skirmishing during this time, but without decisive results. Fearing he would endeavor to pass up the James river towards Richmond from Charles City Courthouse, Hampton took position to prevent this. The Confederates had at this time been reinforced by Chambliss' brigade from W. H. F Lee's division, and by the unattached brigade commanded by General Gary. Sheridan meantime finding himself thus headed off from his intended crossing, made for the river at a landing from which his command could be ferried over by the Federal gunboats, and sent a messenger to Grant asking for reinforcements. But meantime it was necessary to cover the wagon-train and gain time to enable it to reach its destination. From this resulted a sharp fight.

General Gregg with his division was ordered by Sheridan to hold, at all hazards, his position confronting Hampton near Samaria church. He was told he must, without fail, hold it until the wagon-train reached a place of safety. Gregg accordingly fortified his ground and made all preparations to carry out his orders. His troopers and horses had been rested, well fed, and supplied with ample rations at White House, and his numbers had been augmented by recruits. Hampton's force, on the other hand, except the two small brigades mentioned as having just joined his command, had been marching and fighting continuously for sixteen consecutive days; food had been very scarce, and their privations, consequently, severe.

Often the hungry fellows, as they watched their animals browsing on grass, or, in its absence, on any green thing, could not avoid envy, wishing they, too, could graze. The tax on physical strength and the strain on the nervous system had been very great. From casualties and exhaustion the number of effective troopers and horses was much reduced, and it should be remembered that, at the commencement of the expedition, the odds were two to one against them.

Hampton, however, with his keen eye for position, perceived his opportunity and determined to demolish Gregg. He well knew he could rely upon the pluck and endurance of his men, and they, in turn, implicitly trusted him.

It was four o'clock on that hot afternoon of June 24th that Gary's brigade was dismounted and took position near Nance's shop, to operate on the enemy's flank in connection with an attack on his front. As Gary became engaged Chambliss' brigade was thrown forward, and, by a movement handsomely executed, connected with Gary's line, and the two brigades hurled themselves impetuously on the exposed flank. At the same time the whole line in front, under the immediate command of Fitz. Lee, rushed upon the enemy's works. Gregg made a stout resistance from his strong position with a hot fire of breech-loaders and well-served artillery, but after a stiff, though short, fight he was completely routed and forced into a precipitate retreat. Then Hampton brought up the Phillips and Jeff. Davis Legions of his division and charged the fugitives with the sabre. This was done in fine style, men and horses seeming to have quite forgotten fatigue and hunger, and for three miles the pursuit was continued. It was not until ten o'clock at night, and within two and half miles of Charles City Courthouse, that bridle-reins were drawn. There were captured one hundred and fifty-seven prisoners,

Infantry capturing a Federal battery.

including one colonel and twelve commissioned officers, and all the enemy's wounded were left behind where they fell. Gregg's division was badly used up by this affair, and crippled until recruited. The wagon-train, it is true, protected by Torbert's cavalry division and by the infantry reinforcements sent by General Grant and Ben. Butler, was moved from Charles City Courthouse to Douthat's landing, and thence, covered by gunboats, ferried across the river and thus saved; but it was beyond the bounds of possibility for Hampton to prevent this with his small force.

On June 26th Hampton crossed the James river with his division, leaving Fitz. Lee on the north side, and Sheridan completed his crossing two days later.

Thus ended the Trevilian expedition, or campaign, as it is usually termed, and we can now sum up the results.

The purpose was, as stated by General Grant

in his report of July 22, 1865, that Sheridan's cavalry should go "*to Charlottesville and Gordonsville to break up the railroad connection between Richmond and the Shenandoah Valley and Lynchburg.*" These, then, were the specific, admitted objects, and certainly they were not accomplished in whole nor in part. Nor was the James River canal destroyed or injured. The cutting off from Lee's army of the supplies furnished by the Shenandoah Valley was effected during the autumn by Sheridan, when he devastated that region, operating with an army about fifty-five thousand strong against a force numbering little more than a fourth of his own, but in the Trevilian expedition he accomplished absolutely nothing of this. Nor did he bring back Hunter with him, as Grant expected. The facts speak for themselves. Indeed, Sheridan, in his report to his commanding general, says: "*I regret my inability to carry out your instructions.*" The sole result obtained by him was a few rails taken up at Trevilian's station, amounting to nothing.

Of the results accomplished by Hampton, on the other hand, the importance ought to be understood. Grant had just been compelled by Lee to abandon his plan of capturing Richmond by open attacks and had determined to endeavor to reduce it by regular siege. His army, now with the heart taken out of it by all the slaughter of the Wilderness, Spotsylvania, and Cold Harbor, was in no condition to make renewed assaults upon the victorious columns of the Army of Northern Virginia, and must, instead of this, try to starve them out in the trenches by investing Petersburg. To this end, their lines of communication must be effectually severed. Of vital importance in this respect was the destruction of the routes for obtaining food supplies from the direction of the Shenandoah Valley. If this could have been done by Sheridan, the effect upon the campaign just at that juncture might have been fatal, and he would have had free hand to do this if Hampton had not defeated him at Trevilian and driven him off from his objective points.

Allusion has already been made to some of the errors contained in the Federal official reports of this expedition, and it will suffice to say that General Grant's report, being necessarily based solely on information derived from these, and not from his own knowledge, falls, of course, into the same mistakes. Hampton captured 852 prisoners exclusive of the wounded that fell into his hands. The prisoners taken by Sheridan, including wounded and nurses carried off, could not possibly have exceeded 300. Their wounded at Trevilian, removed with them by the Federals, amounted by their own accounts to 500, and 125 wounded were left there, besides numerous dead. By the Federal returns their losses during the Trevilian expedition are officially given as 1512, but this is probably considerably under the actual number of killed, wounded, and captured. The total losses in Hampton's division were under 700, and those in Fitz. Lee's division were very light, as it was not engaged in any severe fighting.

On receiving informatian of the rout of Sheridan at Samaria Church, General Lee wrote to General Hampton the following note :

"Headq'rs A. N. V.,
"June 25th, 1864, 6½ P M.

"General :

"Your note of to-day from Phillips House has just been received. I am rejoiced at your success. I thank you and the officers and men of your command for the gallantry and determination with which they have assaulted Sheridan's forces and caused his expedition to end in defeat. So soon as Sheridan crosses the river, I wish you to join me.

"I am, very respectfully,

Your obt. servant,

"R. E. LEE.

"Major-General Wade Hampton."

And thus the Trevilian cavalry duel was decided, and as it was purely a cavalry fight from first to last, no infantry having the possibility of giving physical or moral support to either side, and as the duration of the movements was sufficient amply to test the ability of the two leaders and the fighting power and endurance of the men, I do not think it is going beyond the inevitable logical sequence to say that the result of an impartial inquiry must confirm the fact that Hampton was proved to be incomparably the abler cavalry general of the two contestants.

CHAPTER VI.

THE WILSON RAID

WHEN Hampton reached the south side of the James river and rejoined his army his command greatly needed rest to recuperate men and horses. But this was not to be.

Petersburg was practically an outwork of Richmond; they must stand or fall together. The line of communication by railroad to the Shenandoah Valley region—the Virginia Central—had been saved by Hampton in the Trevilian expedition. But there were three roads leading to the South. Of these, the Weldon railroad ran nearly due south from Petersburg, and was the first to be exposed to attack, but its seizure would not be fatal while the other two lines were preserved. The Southside, from Petersburg, and the Danville railroad from Richmond, the remaining two lines, having a junction at Burkeville, were covered by the right flank of the Confederate army. A permanent lodgment upon them by the enemy would effect the investment of Petersburg and necessitate its evacuation.

Grant had by this time become convinced of the futility of direct attacks against Lee's fortified positions, and henceforth his chief efforts were to be directed to turning his adversary's right flank, and thus occupying his lines of communication. The Weldon railroad would, of necessity, as we have said, be the object of his first movements. For this purpose, on June 21st, he commenced to swing round to his left to effect a lodgment on that railroad. In this he met a severe check, losing in the two following days' fighting two thousand two hundred prisoners, besides a ghastly list of killed and wounded, and failed altogether in accomplishing his purpose.

On June 21st General James H. Wilson, with his own and Kautz's division of cavalry, numbering together six thousand seven hundred and fourteen "effective mounted men," by the field return of June 20, 1864, started upon an expedition. Kautz was attached to the Army of the James, on the north side of the river, commanded by Ben. Butler, and, consequently, was not nominally attached to Sheridan's corps, but practically had to be reckoned with as part of it, as he could be transferred with rapidity from one side of the river to the other as needed. The object of the expedition was to tear up the rails and permanently cripple the Southside, as well as the Danville railroad near Burkeville junction. These were the orders given to Wilson by Meade, but it was originally intended that he should communicate with Hunter, supposed to be near Lynchburg, and he was to have been entrusted with considerable discretion, including authority to pass over into North Carolina. The plans were based upon the supposition that Sheridan would detain Hampton sufficiently long to enable Wilson to complete his work. Meade writes to Grant to this effect on June 21st:

"Hampton being yesterday at the White House will relieve Wilson of any apprehension of being disturbed, and I trust Sheridan will keep Hampton occupied. Wilson will be instructed, when at the junction, to communicate with Hunter, near Lynchburg."

Wilson had expressed the opinion that he could attain the objects of his proposed expedition provided he was not followed by Hampton. In justice to Wilson it should, therefore, be remembered that he was warranted in believing that such arrangements would be made as were necessary to protect him from

General Hampton's Sword.

"No me saques sin razon,
No me enbaines sin honor."

Hampton, and also that by the time of his return from his raid the Weldon railroad by Reams station would be found occupied by his friends. Sheridan was not expected at headquarters to render any assistance to Wilson, except by keeping Hampton occupied.

On June 22d the raiders passed round the right flank of the Confederate lines near Reams station, and proceeded on their mission. W H. F Lee's division made pursuit, and harassed their movements, interfering to a certain extent with the success of their plans, and doing good fighting. In spite of this, however, they penetrated to the Southside railroad and to Burkeville junction, doing a considerable amount of damage to the railroads. They then made an attempt to destroy the Staunton River bridge, which, if successful, would have caused serious interruption, as it was an important structure, the river being broad and unfordable. In this they were foiled by some local militia, who held a good position on the bridge. From there, Wilson turned back, with the intention of regaining the lines of his army.

In pursuance of orders received from General Lee, Hampton moved off his division on June 27th to endeavor to intercept Wilson, and by noon on the following day reached the neighborhood of Stony Creek station, on the Weldon railroad about ten miles south of Reams station. Having ascertained through scouts the direction by which Wilson was coming, Hampton communicated with General Lee, suggesting that some infantry be sent to Reams station, as he thought the raiders were pointing for that place of crossing, and he also requested that Fitz. Lee with his division be ordered to take position near there, and keep in close communication with him. These dispositions were accordingly made by General Lee. Hampton counted upon meeting Wilson on Sappony creek, a few miles westward, and sent forward

Chambliss' brigade, of W H. F Lee's division, with orders to charge vigorously as soon as the column was met. This was done, and the raiders were driven back to Sappony church, behind which they dismounted and took up a naturally strong position. Chambliss' men were also quickly dismounted, when they in turn were attacked, but held their ground, and their line was then strengthened somewhat and a reinforcement of 200 infantry received. Wilson made endeavors to break through, but without success, and the firing continued during the night. Major Chew had only two guns with him, but these he used with effect. Meantime the Federal commander, thinking he would find his own infantry at Reams station, was very desirous of escaping in that direction, and made his dispositions during the night for that end as far as he could. At daylight, however, Hampton sent Butler with his own and Rosser's brigade round the enemy's left flank. Butler made the necessary detour, threw forward the two brigades dismounted, and Hampton at the same time pressed with his line in front. The result was that the Federals were entirely routed, and broke in various directions in great disorder, leaving dead and wounded behind. The general direction of the larger number was for Reams station. After pursuing them for a couple of miles, taking many prisoners, and dispersing scattered detachments, Hampton drew off towards Stony Creek station with a view of preventing them from getting away by crossing between there and Reams station. The roads were accordingly properly secured to carry out this plan. Two Federal detachments, separated from the main body, were encountered and dealt with summarily by mounted charges. The bridge over Rowanty creek was secured and a third detachment run down, scattered, and broken up. At night a rest was taken near Stony Creek station. This situation was occupied because it was central, enabling the blow to be struck to the north towards Reams station, if the enemy attempted to cross in that direction, or to the south, if they should make for a crossing at Jarratt station. Meantime Hampton was anxiously expecting every moment to receive news from Reams station informing him of what had occurred there, and as to what direction the enemy had taken, if they had not all been captured. Much to his surprise no message was received even during the night.

When Hampton had perceived, after the rout, that the principal portions of Wilson's force were making for Reams station he was well satisfied, for he knew they would there encounter the infantry and Fitz. Lee's division. The raiders, on the other hand, expected to find their own friends established there, but, greatly to their consternation, on reaching the neighborhood of that place, they found themselves confronted by hostile infantry and cavalry. At first, Wilson did not appreciate the strength of the force opposing him, and tried to cut his way through, having closed up his artillery and wagons and ambulances with his main column, which by that time had been to a considerable extent reformed. But finding this impossible, and that he was being enveloped on both flanks, he abandoned all his artillery, consisting of 12 field-guns and 4 howitzers, as well as all his wagons and ambulances, and retreated precipitately back in the direction from which he had come. Disembarrassed from all impediments, without attempting to preserve much organization or maintain ranks, and with neither ability nor intention of further fighting, through woods and by-roads they galloped. Kautz, with a part of his command, became separated from the others, and made off, to the left of Reams station, through the woods in a broken-up condition, and somehow got through to the lines of his army. Wilson made a long detour at a very rapid rate, and going round Stony Creek station much to the west of it, and continuing to dash on without stoppage during the night, crossed the Nottoway river near Jarratt, some ten miles south of Stony Creek station, and eventually reached his army in an exhausted and very disorganized state.

Meantime Hampton had bivouacked his two divisions, as stated, near Stony Creek station, giving the men a necessary rest, as they had been under fire during the previous night. Every moment he had been looking for the information which should have been despatched to him from the cavalry at Reams station, but none came. By gray dawn the troopers were in marching order, but still not one word had been received concerning the result of the fighting at Reams station, so that it was impossible to divine the position of the enemy or of Fitzhugh Lee's division. At nine o'clock on the morning of June 30th a note was received addressed to the "Commanding Officer of the Troops at Stony Creek depot," from Fitzhugh Lee, saying that he was "still pursuing the enemy, capturing prisoners, etc.," and that he was five miles from Nottoway river, on the Hicksford road. The note went on to say that he thought "the enemy, after crossing the river, will try to cross the railroad at Jarratt depot," and that he wished "all the available force sent to that point to intercept their march, until he got up." Hampton immediately moved his command on Jarratt, but when he had arrived within five miles of that place his scouts, who had been sent ahead, reported to him that the enemy had passed there at daylight. A rapid march was made to endeavor still to cut them off from their lines, but it was too late. With proper concert of action between the cavalry at Reams station and Hampton, that is to say, if the latter had been informed in the usual way by his officer in command there, nothing could have prevented the capture of Wilson and all the troops then with him.

There were captured by Hampton 806 prisoners on the day of the Sappony church engagement, and about 500 more were taken at Reams station. All the artillery, twelve guns and four howitzers, and the wagons and ambulances of Wilson, fell into the hands of the Confederates, as has been said. The Federal reports state that they had taken from the farmers along the route of their raid some 5,000 horses. This is probably an overestimate, but whatever the number was, they were all recovered, and this is also true of much private property, consisting of household furniture, vehicles, and personal articles. In one of the wagons taken was found a silver communion service belonging to St. John's church, in Lunenburg county. The pillaging had been so extensive that much attention was attracted to the subject, and an investigation was instituted at Federal headquarters. The generals concerned admitted the facts, and expressed great regret, attributing the robberies to an organized system existing among the men. It was observed that Kautz's division had for a long time served under Ben. Butler.

Besides the 1,300 prisoners lost by Wilson, there were numerous dead and wounded left on the field. But this, though bad enough, was not the worst of it for him, for the demoralization produced by the mode of their escape was even more damaging to his troops than the losses. It required a long time and much recruiting to bring Wilson's division back to a state of efficiency, and the command of Kautz never recovered. Hampton's losses were insignificant, being only two killed, eighteen wounded, and two missing in his own division, and those of the other divisions were quite small, but I have not the exact figures.

The destruction wrought by Wilson's raid, though overestimated by him, was important for the moment, but not of lasting injury, the railroads being rapidly repaired. Even by most Federal authorities it is stated that the results accomplished by no means compensated for the losses sustained by the raiders, which must have considerably exceeded one-fourth of the 6,714 men with which the expedition started, to say nothing of the even more serious damage suffered from demoralization. The temporary inconvenience experienced by Lee from the injury to these railroads would, of course, have been very much greater if his line of communication by the Virginia Central railroad had not been preserved by Hampton.

After the rout of Sappony church, General Hampton led Chambliss' brigade in some of the charges made on detachments encountered. Two flags were captured on one of these occasions by members of the Ninth Virginia, and the men greatly wished to present these colors to their leader. It was the rule, however, to turn over captured property to the authorities, and these flags were therefore forwarded to the War Department, but from there were sent back to General Hampton, accompanied by a very complimentary letter from General Lee. It is needless to say they never were recaptured, but carefully preserved as a memento of a well-fought field, and also of the kind feelings and bravery of his followers.

On the morning of June 29th the last of Sheridan's force had crossed the James river, and on the evening of that day moved out towards Reams station to endeavor to assist Wilson. They were too late, however, for this purpose, and even if they had arrived sooner were in no condition at that time to try conclusions.

Thus were frustrated the expeditions intended to destroy the Virginia Central railroad and the roads south of the James. The entire losses in killed, wounded, and missing in Hampton's division, from the commencement of the Trevilian expedition until the final dispersion of the Wilson raid, amounted to seven hundred and nineteen, including twenty-one casualties in Chew's batteries of horse artillery, and the losses in Fitz. Lee's division were so small as not to swell the aggregate number materially.

The results above referred to were obtained by Hampton with a proportionately very small force acting against the three divisions of Sheridan's corps and the division of Kautz, which latter had to be reckoned with as practically a part of the Army of the Potomac, as has been before observed, as much as if it had belonged to Sheridan's corps. Not only had this been accomplished, but also the four Federal divisions named had been so roughly handled and so much reduced in numbers and *morale* that they were placed in a state of enforced quiescence for nearly six weeks until largely recruited, and in fact never again during the campaign of 1864 were as formidable or effective as before. <u>Never again did this cavalry make any serious effort to interfere with Lee's communications.</u> The losses in Hampton's command had been small in proportion to that of the enemy, and its *morale* could not have been better. Throughout all the fighting and privations endured, the men never failed to appreciate that they were handled both with excellent judgment as well as with brilliancy, and that every life lost or wound received was the price paid for a more than compensating military advantage; that for each was obtained a *quid pro quo*. But, more than this, they knew Hampton for what he was. His amiable disposition and attractive manners—always dignified and military, but kindly, frank, and gracious—imbued all those under his command with a personal feeling of attachment. He seemed to be acquainted with every private, remembering faces and names in a wonderful manner; and it also used to be said he knew every horse in the corps. It is certain he would often notice when a man was riding an animal other than his own, and inquire of him the reason. Besides this, his great personal gallantry and individual prowess—his figure always to be seen in the front—the sharing of fatigue and privations, the victories, which his presence seemed to make assured, caused among his soldiers that sentiment of devoted loyalty which comes only to good fighters serving under a born leader of men. Amidst the tramp of the horses, the crack of the rifles, and the roar of artillery, they would, at sight of their General, feel that inspiration which for the time being exalts ordinary men into heroes.

CHAPTER VII.

PICKETING—SHERIDAN TRANSFERRED TO COMMAND IN THE SHENANDOAH VALLEY—DIVISION COMMANDERS ORDERED TO REPORT DIRECT TO HAMPTON—CHANGE OF STAFF.

AFTER the operations just described, there were no events of sufficient importance to relate until the early part of August was reached. In the meantime, however, there was skirmishing frequently, and two somewhat sharp brushes, but the Federal cavalry did not venture much beyond their infantry. Everything practicable was done to recruit the horses of Hampton's command, but the mode of procuring remounts, as before explained, was the weakest feature in the system. Picketing there was, of course, and plenty of it,

A night's rest. Typical scene in a Confederate Cavalry camp

then and throughout the campaign, and this is a duty the cavalry dislike far more than fighting. Not only are there hardships and loneliness on post, but annoyances and dangers without excitement, or credit to be gained. One instance, a very ordinary occurrence, may serve to give some idea of what is meant. Long after this, in the early winter, a detachment of cavalry was picketing the extreme lines near Stony creek. There was one post at which about this time two videttes had been murdered at night. The term "murdered" is hardly incorrect, for to take a life secretly and wantonly, without military purpose or special justification, is morally murder, at least in the estimation of an intended victim. Naturally this post was not a favorite, and it may have been a compliment, but it was a disagreeable one, to be assigned to it. So thought a trooper as he took his station there one night at about ten o'clock, to remain four hours before being relieved. It was literally "pitch-dark," the post being in the midst of a wood with a ravine on the right separating it from the other stations. There was a light, chilly rain falling, and as the man, wet and uncomfortable, sat rigid on his perfectly motionless horse, whose ears he was unable to see, he could not help thinking that it was just the night to be sitting in a dry room, however rough, before burning logs, with a tumbler of hot whiskey, "though lost to sight, to mem'ry dear," beside him, and a pipe in his mouth, and also how snug it would feel covered up with plenty of blankets in a clean, warm, soft bed, hearing the music of the rain-drops on the roof. It was perfectly still, except for the faint sound of the rain upon the dead leaves. After an hour or more all such reflections as the above were effectually dispelled, for, from the direction of the ravine, he detected a slight noise, altogether different from that of the rain. It was a stealthy footstep on the wet ground.

Quite wide awake now, he listened intently, and there was no doubt that the cause of the sound was gradually coming nearer to him. It was evident, he thought, that if he was not to play the rôle of number three in murdered videttes, it was high time to take a hand in arranging the programme. To fire on the newcomer would not serve the purpose, for, if his shot missed, as it probably would in the darkness, his exact position would be perceived and taken advantage of, or, if the unwelcome visitor made off, the picket-post would be turned out on hearing the report of the gun, and no evidence of the presence of an enemy being discovered, there would have been a laugh at his expense for being "skeered at nothin'" So the vidette noiselessly slipped off his horse on the left side, took a stand just behind the animal, and quietly drew his sabre. Rifle and pistol, loaded with paper cartridges, might snap in the wet weather, but, as Pat says of his shillalah, the sabre "never misses fire." Shortening his arm, ready to drive the point with a will, he waited patiently for the stranger to develop his tactics. He inferred the murderer would think him seated in the saddle, and as soon as the exact position of the horse was ascertained, would leap upon his supposed victim with a knife, and then would be the moment to show the counter-stroke by running him through the body. For a few seconds the sounds ceased altogether, but then commenced again approaching, the unseen person even more cautious than before. At length he stopped, remaining quite still, and must have been almost within reach of the horse; probably was groping about with his hands feeling for him. The trooper now felt confident the assassin was within reach, and was about to thrust with his sword, but restrained his impatience, thinking to be absolutely certain of his man if he awaited the misdirected attack which he expected. Just then the horse, who up to that moment had remained as still as the grave, moved slightly. At this, whoever it was glided quickly away towards the ravine, and thus ended the incident. The vidette was very much annoyed at this, blaming himself for allowing the wretch to escape to ply his nefarious occupation with more success, perhaps, some other night.

On August 2d General Sheridan was relieved of the command of the cavalry of the Potomac and ordered to the Shenandoah Valley. Thus was completed his four months of service at the head of the cavalry corps, and from this date his career does not concern our narrative, but the results obtained by him during this time are a pertinent subject for discussion.

In April, Sheridan had taken command of a fine body of cavalry, the bequest of Pleasanton, in numbers and equipment almost absurdly out of proportion to the force available for Hampton. General Grant gave him every opportunity to distinguish himself with a free hand. But during the progress of the "overland campaign" it is not apparent where he succeeded very well in veiling the movements of his own infantry or in unmasking those of his enemies. He made a dash to capture Richmond with a force which would seem not to have been inadequate, but failed to make any impression. His operations against Lee's lines of communication had no important effect, and were costly to his own command. Grant's lines of communication on land were so fully guarded by infantry as to afford him no occupation. He fought well, but always found his match in fighting, and much more than his match as to strategy in Hampton, and his losses were, proportionately, very large. In fact, he was far, indeed, from being a master of strategy, and whatever he succeeded in accomplishing, so far as his career against the Army of Northern Virginia is concerned, was done by sheer weight of greatly superior numbers. In his report, which was made some time subsequently, of his operations from May 4th to August 1st, he remarks that his command did as heavy fighting as the infantry, and that the casualties were as great in proportion. In another place he says he thinks his losses did not exceed six thousand, which is somewhat more than appears from the compiled returns, but these latter, from causes already mentioned, cannot be considered correct. But even if his losses did in fact only amount to six thousand, they still about equalled in number the entire force with which Hampton fought him. He also says his campaign effected "the almost total annihilation of the rebel cavalry." How wide of the mark this is, the reader can judge from the facts related, as well as when he adds: "I am led to believe, on information derived from reliable sources, that the enemy's cavalry was superior to ours in numbers." Of course, every effort was made by the Confederates to mislead him as to their small force, and bogus information from pretended prisoners, and other reports intended to deceive, seem to have served to effectt his purpose, but the actual numbers available for Hampton are now matter of record.

On August 11th the following order was issued :

"Headq'rs Dep't Nor. Va.,
"11th August, 1864.
"(Extract.)
"Special Order' No. 189.

"VII. Maj.-Gen'l Wade Hampton is assigned to the command of the cavalry of this army.

"Division commanders will report to him accordingly

"By command of
"GENERAL R. E. LEE.
"W H. TAYLOR,
"A. A. Gen'l."

General Wade Hampton of the wars of 1776 and 1812. The grandfather of General Hampton

(261)

This requires some explanation. After Major-General J. E. B. Stuart received his death-wound on May 11, 1864, Hampton, as Senior Major-General of cavalry, took command of the corps, as has been stated in a former part of this narrative. During Stuart's life-time all the divisions, unless detached on special service, had reported to and received orders from corps headquarters. When Hampton took command the system in this respect was changed, the generals of divisions reporting to army headquarters, except when engaged in actual movements under the personal direction of the corps commander. The disadvantages to the service, and the sources of embarrassment to the corps commander, which would naturally be produced by this change are obvious, and it requires but little "reading between the lines" in the accounts given of operations to perceive that on important occasions the extent of successes was diminished from this cause. One would indeed anticipate that this change would practically neutralize, to a great extent, the advantages of corps organization, and disintegrate a command measurably into divisional composition. Instead of a compact unit, as a corps should be, with division commanders directly controlled by a single will, through which celerity of action, the essence of cavalry usefulness, is obtained, there is a risk, at times, of a division of wills, and it is a homely but true saying that "too many cooks spoil the broth." It is not advisable, at this late day, to discuss how this change happened to be brought about, or by whom, but it is necessary to understand clearly that it was not occasioned by any wish on the part of General Lee to curtail Hampton's sphere of authority, and the order of August 11th quoted above, which undid the wrong, is a proof of this. The relations between these two generals were always of the most friendly and cordial nature, and it is not the least of the pleasures derived from reading their correspondence to observe the entire confidence Lee reposed in Hampton's ability, and how he relied more and more upon his gallantry, skill, and good judgment, as this most exacting of campaigns progressed.

In connection with the order of August 11th came the assignment to Hampton of the staff attached to the headquarters of the cavalry when Stuart commanded, and this necessitated his parting with all but three of his military family—Lowndes, Taylor, and Preston Hampton—the others continuing on the divisional staff under General M. C. Butler. His new staff consisted of able officers and agreeable gentlemen, but nevertheless the separation from old and tried friends could not but be a wrench. His chief of staff, Major Theodore G. Barker, A. A. G., had been close to him since the commencement of the war, having been adjutant of the Hampton Legion, in the organization of which he was largely concerned, and with whose conduct on the field he was conspicuously associated. When General Hampton was transferred to the cavalry in 1862, Barker had accompanied him as adjutant of the "First brigade," and was engaged in the brilliant operations of that command, and had become adjutant of the division, when his General was assigned to one.

CHAPTER VIII.

CHANGES IN THE FEDERAL AND CONFEDERATE CAVALRY FORCES, AND THE NUMBERS OF EACH—ENGAGEMENTS OF AUGUST 16TH AND 17TH ON THE NORTH SIDE OF THE JAMES—BUTLER'S SUCCESS ON AUGUST 23D AT REAMS STATION—BATTLE OF REAMS STATION ON AUGUST 25TH.

WHEN Sheridan went to the Shenandoah Valley the First division (Torbert) of cavalry of the Army of the Potomac accompanied him, and on August 17th the Third division (Wilson) was also sent there. The Second division (Gregg) remained with the army. This division, after all its heavy losses, was recruited, and numbered present for duty in September, according to the official report of that date, 4,670. Kautz's division, at that time about 2,000 strong, though nominally attached to the Army of the James, practically increased the force opposed to Hampton. Besides this, there were bodies of unattached cavalry with the Army of the James, which swelled the odds against him still more. The facilities possessed by Grant of transferring troops easily from one bank of the James river to the other by means of pontoon bridges and steamers rendered his cavalry as well as infantry quickly available on either side desired. General Grant, in September, estimates his available cavalry at 9,000, but General Meade thinks these two divisions, exclusive of the unattached, numbered much less. It is surprising how inaccurately the accounts were kept, and how little reliance can be placed on them. Fitzhugh Lee's division was detached and sent to the Valley of the Shenandoah early in August. The two divisions which remained with the Army of Northern Virginia, by the monthly return of August 31st, are credited with 5,344 men, but many of these were without horses, and others had unserviceable ones, owing to the wretched system for remounting already referred to, and thus the effective strength was greatly reduced. On September 27th Rosser's brigade was also sent to the Shenandoah Valley, thus further reducing the corps. It should be remembered that the words "present for duty" in the Confederate monthly or other reports meant all the men in camp, whether provided with horses or dismounted. It may also be repeated that many returns in the published "Records of the Union and Confederate Armies" are incorrect, as for instance the return of September 10, 1864, in which Lomax's division of cavalry appears as part of Hampton's corps, whereas such was never the case, as it was in the Shenandoah Valley. Dearing's brigade was at first unattached, but served under Hampton frequently in the late summer or autumn. Gary's brigade was unattached, and served with the Richmond-defence troops north of the James, and not with Hampton, unless he was incidentally in their neighborhood. Thus the Federal cavalry remaining with the army greatly exceeded Hampton's force, but during the rest of the campaign they kept close to their infantry, and accomplished, and in fact attempted, no separate enterprises. The Confederate cavalry were able to keep them in bounds and at the same time do much useful work in connection with the infantry as well as on their own account. It is not the purpose of this narrative to give a detailed account of their services, but only to describe some of their movements.

On August 11th General Hampton received a confidential communication from General Lee, directing him to move his division, General Butler commanding, to Culpeper to take part in a contemplated demonstration in that quarter, having reference to the Valley. He accordingly crossed the river and marched in that direction, but on August 14th received a telegram from Lee recalling him, as the plan had been changed and he was wanted near Richmond. By ten o'clock on the morning of August 16th he reached White Tavern, eight miles from Richmond, on the Charles City road, and following the maxim of Napoleon by pressing forward towards the sounds of heavy fire, was in time to support W H. F Lee, who was seriously engaged, having been ordered to the north of the James river on August 14th to meet the enemy's advance. As soon as Grant had thoroughly fortified his lines in front of Petersburg, he could leave sufficient force there to hold them and yet spare troops to strive to edge round to the left to effect a lodgment on the Weldon railroad leading South, in carrying out the programme which he had laid down for himself, as already explained. At the same time he would transfer troops to the north side of the James to make a demonstration there in connection with that on the south side of the river, hoping thus to gain an advantage on one side or the other; perhaps to capture Richmond by a dash before Lee could come up in force. He was occupied in one of these double movements now, besides having the object of deterring Lee from reinforcing Early in the Valley, and had reached on the north side within eight miles of Richmond.

W H. F Lee was hard pressed by a much superior force, chiefly infantry. He was forced back somewhat, and Brigadier-General Chambliss, commanding one of his brigades, was killed while gallantly rallying his men an excellent officer, whose death was a great loss to the army. Just at this critical juncture Hampton's division (now Butler's) came upon the scene, and was moved, dismounted, to the right and rear of the enemy, and W H. F Lee with his division and Gary's brigade attacked in front. The result was a speedy success, regaining the lost ground and driving the enemy beyond. Some prisoners, mostly infantry, were taken. On the following day General Lee determined to attack on the front, having by that time, in consequence of the delay effected, got up enough men for the purpose. In this the cavalry participated, W H. F Lee's division in front and Butler's turning the right flank. The enemy were driven back, breastworks captured, and one hundred and sixty-seven prisoners taken by the cavalry. That night the enemy retreated, and Hampton, in pursuance of orders, took up his former position on the south side of the river.

General Lee's official communication to General Hampton about these operations was highly commendatory, and in it he says: "I desire to express the gratification I have derived from the conduct of the cavalry during its late operations north of James river * * Please express to the officers and men my thanks for their gallant and valuable services."

General Chambliss had fallen, as has been mentioned, just as W. H. F Lee's line had been forced back before Hampton's arrival, and he died in the enemy's hands. He had been buried by them in a wooden coffin, and the grave carefully marked with his name and rank. His friends, under flag of truce, after that day's fighting was over, requested that the body be returned to them. It was accordingly exhumed and brought back to them under flag of truce. All this was considerately and kindly done, and it is therefore pleasant to record it.

When Hampton returned to the south side of the James river the enemy had obtained a foot-hold on the Weldon railroad, their first step in severing that artery of supply for the Army of Northern Virginia. They held the road

Pitz. Simons house, Hasel street, Charleston, S. C., birthplace of General Hampton

from near Petersburg down to Reams station, from which latter point Hancock intended to destroy the road farther south. In moving down Butler's division to occupy the picket-line previously held in front of Reams station, the enemy was encountered at Monck's Neck bridge, about two miles west of the station, on Rowanty creek. Here, on August 23d, Butler attacked the position with his invariable determination, and after a stiff fight drove the enemy, a division of infantry, into the cover of their works at Reams station, and established his picket-line, with a loss of twenty-one killed, one hundred and three wounded, and twelve missing. The movement was skillfully managed and gallantly carried out, and led to important results, as will be seen, for it suggested to Hampton the feasibility of capturing Reams station. A careful reconnoissance of the ground was made, and a plan of attack was submitted by Hampton to General Lee, of which the latter approved, and Lieutenant-General A. P Hill, with Heth's division, was assigned to the work in connection with Hampton. The cavalry consisted of W H. F Lee's division, Barringer just then commanding, and Butler's division. To the latter's old brigade about this time General Dunovant had been assigned. General Rosser, though not entirely recovered from his wound received at Trevilian, was again conspicuously at the head of the "Laurel brigade."

General Hill's infantry was quietly conducted by the cavalry through the country to Monck's Neck bridge, where a halt was made for the night, and the plan of attack agreed upon. The following is the account of the part taken by the cavalry in the action on August 25th:

It was arranged that Hampton, with the main part of his force, should strike the left flank of the enemy on the Weldon railroad, and, with the rest, cover the approach of

General Hill on Reams station. The proper dispositions having been made, Hampton crossed with the attacking force at Malone's bridge, and soon encountered the enemy's pickets, which were, by a mounted charge, driven in on his cavalry, which were then forced back out of a favorable position towards Reams station, but not until after a stiff dismounted fight. A section of McGregor's battery did fine execution during this movement. The enemy was thus compelled to bring up infantry to replace his cavalry, and accordingly deployed a heavy force, endeavoring to envelop both of Hampton's flanks, but this he was prevented from effecting. The troops instinctively followed the directions once given by General Butler to one of his colonels, who requested reinforcements on the ground of being flanked. Said he:

"Well! Flank them back, then!"

General Hill was now notified of the position of affairs, and it was suggested that he attack.

This he said he would do, and requested Hampton to move back his line somewhat, as if withdrawing, so as to induce the enemy to follow down the railroad, enabling him to take them in rear. This manœuvre Hampton executed, retiring about 400 yards, but the Federals followed with very great caution. At five o'clock P M. General Hill's artillery opened, thus announcing his advance, and General Hampton at once ordered forward his whole line, which was formed across the railroad on the west. The enemy was driven to his works at Reams station and some minor outworks taken. Finding that General Hill was pressing the Federals from the west into Reams station works, Hampton brought his line to the east side of the railroad, keeping his left flank on the road and swinging his right round so as to take the enemy engaged with Hill in rear The ground to be traversed, very difficult naturally, had been further obstructed by felled trees and other impediments, but the cavalry, dismounted, pushed forward with a spirit entitling them to march shoulder to shoulder with the infantry of the Army of Northern Virginia, and there is no higher praise than this. When all of the enemy had been driven from the outerworks into the fortifications at Reams station, they made a still more stubborn fight. Previous to this, they would retreat from one minor point to make a stand at another, and so on back towards the main works. It was during this time that some of the men had much sport with a little "Dutchman." This fellow was as fat as a beer-barrel, not much over five feet in height, with very short legs and pudgy body, and could hardly run, in spite of his best efforts, faster than a jog-trot. Each time, as he would be flushed out of a place with his comrades, he would work his little legs as best he could, moving his arms grotesquely like a windmill, blowing like a porpoise and perspiring in streams, but quite unable to keep up with his better conditioned companions. It was such a laughable sight that the men good-naturedly refrained from shooting him, but every time he was jumped would chaff him with jokes, and "Go it, Dutchy." Probably he was one of the "cheap substitutes" of which Grant was about that time complaining to Stanton as sent him by the "loyal" of the North; often becoming "too willing prisoners," he said.

The check received when the enemy occupied his main works was but of short duration, and with a yell which must have sent mortal terror to the heart of "little Dutchy," if still in the land of the living, the cavalry rushed across the breastworks; the day was won. They then took charge of the trenches, and the infantry were relieved. The fighting had lasted for twelve hours. The cavalry captured 781 prisoners, besides sixty-six badly wounded, and buried 143 dead. Their own losses were only sixteen killed and seventy-eight wounded, and no prisoners lost. They captured six caissons, very many small arms, and three flags, besides other property. Their loss was surprisingly small in proportion to the fire sustained, the shooting of the Federals being unusually wild, the bullets ranging very high, a sure sign of want of skill or nerve. It was a sin to waste so much good ammunition. Perhaps this was caused by the recent receipt of a shipment of food for gunpowder purchased abroad, of which the "little Dutchy" just described may have been a sample. The total captures of the combined cavalry and infantry amounted to 2,150 prisoners, seven stand of colors, nine pieces of artillery, and 3,150 small arms and stores. As Lieutenant-General A. P Hill expressed it in writing of this engagement, "The sabre and the bayonet have shaken hands on the enemy's captured breastworks."

This was an important operation. It is true

that the Federals succeeded in effecting by perseverance and numbers a permanent lodgment on the Weldon railroad, thus severing that line of communication with the South, and compelling the Confederates later on to wagon from Stony Creek station. But in the fight of Reams station they received a serious discouraging set-back in their programme, and time was thus gained by Lee. Among the infantry engaged was General James Conner's brigade, of Wilcox's division, and it must have been pleasant to that gallant soldier and lovable gentleman to have literally "shaken hands on the enemy's captured breastworks" with his old preceptor in the art of war, for he had made his *debut* in the Hampton Legion at the first battle of Manassas (Bull Run).

General Lee, in his report of this affair to the War Department, says: "One line of breastworks was carried by the cavalry under Hampton with great gallantry."

Under date of August 26th General Lee writes to General Hampton as follows:

"Your note has been received. I am very much gratified with the success of yesterday's operations. I wished you to be near there, because I feared that as Gregg was so much in the background in yesterday's operations he might be preparing for a raid on the Danville and Southside railroads. I wish you now to rest the two divisions as much as practicable, and to take such position as would enable you most speedily to intercept and punish any party which they might send out against our communications."

In writing to Governor Vance, of North Carolina, about this battle, General Lee says that the men "advanced through a thick abatis of felled trees under a heavy fire of musketry and artillery and carried the enemy's works with a steady courage, which elicited the warm commendations of their corps and division commanders and the admiration of the army," and adds : "The operations of the cavalry were not less distinguished for boldness and efficiency than those of the infantry."

It was General Hancock who commanded the Federals this day, and the mortification felt at the result by that brave, proud soldier was intense. It is reported by his friends that he said on the field he would rather have died than have witnessed his corps in such a rout.

CHAPTER IX.

THE CATTLE-RAID—THE SCOUTS.

NEAR Coggin's Point, on the James river, less than five miles east of City Point and opposite to Westover, was a large herd of cattle belonging to the Army of the Potomac. From information obtained by trusty scouts Hampton ascertained the exact location of these beeves and the disposition of the Federal troops in the vicinity, and decided that he could capture the herd. To accomplish this it would be necessary to make an incursion in the rear of the Federal army, and to within almost rifle-shot of City Point. Now, City Point was the headquarters and base of the Army of the Potomac. Here, General

Grant and his military family were "at home" to visitors, but did not look for a call from Hampton. It was supposed to be as safe as Washington. The good people at Boston would have been no more surprised by a raid made to carry away Plymouth Rock than was the Federal army by the rummaging of their larder under the very nose of headquarters. It was no wonder that their nerves were badly shaken, and this they certainly were. The unexpected had happened to them.

On the morning of September 14th Hampton moved out upon the expedition from his position south of Petersburg. He took with him W. H. F. Lee's division, Rosser's and Dearing's brigades, and 100 men from Young's and Dunovant's brigades. Proceeding southeasterly down the west side of Rowanty creek on a swift march, he bivouacked quietly for the night at Wilkinson's bridge, and, making an early start next morning, bearing nearly north, reached during the day Cook's bridge on the Blackwater river. This detour brought him round the left flank of the Federals, nearly due south of Coggin's Point, and only about ten miles from where he intended to break through their picket-guards. The bridge at this point had been destroyed, as he was aware, and he selected the place for crossing the river for this reason, as he would not be looked for from that direction. In a few hours a temporary bridge was constructed by the engineers, the horses meantime rested and fed, and by midnight the river was crossed and the march resumed. North of the Blackwater about nine miles, near Sycamore church, was the largest detachment of the enemy nearest to the herd of cattle, which was about two miles farther on. To the right and left of this point were smaller bodies of Federals. So Hampton determined to attack the largest force first and scatter it, and head off the smaller detachments, thus preventing concentration. To Rosser was accordingly assigned the central attack, after accomplishing which he was to proceed to appropriate and carry away the prospective beefsteaks. To W H. F. Lee's division was entrusted the task of driving away the force to the left, and holding the roads leading from City Point from which interference was to be expected. Dearing was to place his brigade on the right of Sycamore church, and when he heard the firing there, was to dash into and demolish a post about three miles from Fort Powhatan, on the James river, and hold the roads leading to the fort to prevent attack from that quarter. At five o'clock A. M., Rosser attacked. The videttes were driven in, but the main body, a regiment, the First District of Columbia cavalry, rallied behind barricades in very good style. However, Rosser lost no time, but made short work of them, annihilating the regiment, all not killed, wounded, or captured making off in every direction, spreading consternation throughout the neighborhood and exaggerated accounts of the numbers of the raiders. As soon as W H. F Lee's and Dearing's people heard the firing, they commenced their part of the programme, dispersing or riding down everything they met. They then held the roads, as directed, thus preventing assistance being sent to the central post, and drove away or took all the couriers whom they could lay hands on. Rosser sent forward a detachment to secure the cattle, which they quickly did, overpowering the guard of 120 men and the herdsmen. Many horses were also taken, eleven wagons, three flags, and the beeves, numbering 2,468. Three camps were burned, a considerable quanity of valuable stores and blankets carried off, and more destroyed. All this was no easy matter, but it was thoroughly done in a business-like manner, without undue haste yet without loss of time. Everything had been well arranged beforehand,

and was carried out without a mistake. The troopers became for the occasion amateur cowboys, and good ones, too. The cavalry, the army's maid of all work, filling the gaps in the military household, were one day storming a battery through abatis and brush, and another driving oxen. The Federal herders of the cattle proved very useful, and served their new masters as well and apparently as readily as if these had been their original employers. When the oxen would become troublesome, showing an inclination to stray into the fields and make delay, the herders, cracking their long lashes, sounding like pistol-shots, would quickly bring them back, though it must be confessed a trooper always rode alongside with a handy weapon to insure loyalty. But everything ran smoothly, and the sight would have gladdened the heart of a Highland chieftain of the olden time, but his best "lift" would have been insignificant compared to this.

Such a mass of cattle kept together would have been unwieldy, perhaps impracticable to manage, but by breaking them up into detachments, with intervals between each, this difficulty was avoided. Completely successful in executing his plans, Hampton commenced to withdraw by 8 o'clock A. M.

While all this was going on in most cheerful manner for the raiders, the greatest consternation and bewilderment were prevailing at Federal headquarters. By prearrangement with General Lee, at the hour at which Hampton attacked, a demonstration to distract attention was made along a part of the line of the army, the infantry driving the enemy's pickets into the fortifications west of the Jerusalem plankroad, and bodies of troops were moved about, as if for a general attack. At the same time Butler, with his cavalry division, began to make himself very disagreeable to the troops in his vicinity. It seemed from all this as if General

Lee was going on the war-path in earnest, and that Hampton's cavalry raid was intended only to distract attention from this, whilst in fact just the reverse was true.

So, Federal headquarters made the wires hot with telegrams, and couriers were sent galloping for dear life with despatches. Meade's "household troops" were kept very busy that day. General Grant was temporarily absent at Harper's Ferry consulting with Sheridan, then in the Shenandoah Valley, but he had a very unpleasant quarter of an hour, and several of them, on receipt of excited telegrams from Meade and from his chief of staff, Humphreys. And poor Kautz, such of his cavalry as had been met by Hampton having been demolished and sent scurrying in all directions, was sadly shattered in nerves, and worrying unlucky Meade with messages and queries, in the replies to which one can almost fancy he hears the General swearing. Many of these telegrams and despatches are preserved in the published records of the War Office. They are entertaining reading even at this late day, for being sent on the spur of the moment amidst all the excitement and exasperation, when there was no time to weigh words, they exhibit the true state of mind of the senders. Like spoken words stored hot in a phonograph, and now released, they seem very different from official despatches prepared carefully after all the hurly-burly is past and blood is cool. Meade evidently believed Lee was advancing in force, and was much worried at the absence of Grant at such a trying time, involving so great responsibility. Kautz sends a message that he has information Hampton's force is 14,000 (!) strong. Sharpe, deputy provost-marshal, says it is Hampton's entire cavalry corps. "Trusty citizens" report an immense force. Meade estimates 6,000. Humphreys, chief of staff, informs Kautz that he can reinforce him with a division of infantry and a battery of artillery, but by that time the bird is flown. Sharpe and the rest fear the capture and destruction of all the immense stores at and around City Point, and put their heads together to arrange to have gun boats rushed up to cover City Point with artillery. The alarm really became almost pathetic.

But Hampton pursued the even tenor of his way. Having procured nice beefsteaks at a convenient market without the trouble of payment, he intended to take them safely home to cook. He retired towards the Blackwater river, and before reaching the stream had reunited all the portions of his command and then quietly crossed. Rosser was sent forward from there to hold the Jerusalem plank-road at a point about thirteen miles south of Petersburg and east of the Weldon railroad. Here he was attacked by Gregg and Kautz with their cavalry, but easily repelled them. So he held the road,

The beefsteak raid, Prince George County, Va.

and the cattle were sent two miles in the rear to the south, and were safely got across the Nottoway river at Freeman's ford, and all brought "home." When Hampton had made sure that the cattle and other spoil were safely out of reach of recapture, he turned his attention to cutting off a goodly portion of the Federal cavalry, but by the time he had made dispositions to get in their rear for this purpose, it was found they had retreated, and this plan was therefore abandoned. So, weary but jolly, his men returned to the bivouac on Rowanty creek. That night, and for many a day afterwards, there were plenty of sardines and other canned food, pickles, and many things esteemed luxuries by poor fellows who had eaten nothing but bacon and flour, and too little of them, for months past. These were picked up by the men in the burned camps, the regularly captured property being turned over to the proper authorities. They had marched 100 miles in three days. The prisoners captured amounted to 304, and Hampton's losses to 10 killed, 47 wounded, and 4 missing.

In writing to General Grant after the affair is over, and the beeves irrevocably lost, Meade is evidently still very much disconcerted. He has discovered, by that time, it was only a cattle-raid, and not part of a general attack, and gives the best excuse he can think of for the loss, with "tears in his voice." He attributes Hampton's success and safe withdrawal to his force being 6,000 men, and he says his own troops were only 3,000 cavalry and 3,000 infantry available, but in fact, to arrive at this estimate of 6,000 for the Confederates, he has used the multiple two. The estimates greatly and drolly varied: from Kautz, 14,000 (!); from Major Van Rensalaer, 5,000; Humphreys says three brigades of cavalry; Sharpe, the whole cavalry corps, and so on. Grant in a despatch to Meade calls the captures "a rich haul," and so they were. Those 2,468 beeves were a Godsend to the army—"Hampton's steaks," as they were termed—and thriftily used lasted for many a week. They were fine, large oxen.

It is amusing to discover now, from the telltale despatches preserved, how nervous during the rest of the campaign the troops were who guarded the lines near City Point, especially in the vicinity of Sycamore church, where Hampton had broken through. They were always hearing strange noises at night, suggested by former unpleasant experiences: sometimes it would be phantom bridge-builders spanning the Blackwater; at others, the tramp in the dark of ghostly horses and the clatter of sabres. Altogether they had a very trying time of it, like children in bed in the dark, and their officers were greatly disgusted by some prompt retreats of their men from imaginary onslaughts, and were thus betrayed into using naughty words.

On General Hampton's return to his quarters he received a note from General Lee, in which he writes:

"I have received your report of the result of your operations, and beg to express my high appreciation of the skill and boldness you have displayed, and my gratification at your handsome and valuable success. You will please convey to the officers and men of your command my thanks for the courage and energy with which they have executed your orders, by which they have added another to the list of important services rendered by the cavalry during the present campaign."

The information about the herd of beeves, upon which the expedition for its capture was arranged, was obtained from Sergeant Shadbourne, of the Jeff. Davis Legion, a scout. He accompanied Rosser's leading regiment as guide, and was foremost in the attack. Sergeant Hogan, in charge of Butler's scouts, was also with the expedition, and did excellent service. One scout was killed and three wounded in the fighting. The scouts of the army did not constitute a distinct organization, but suitable men volunteering for this duty were detailed from the different commands. The position required not only coolness, courage, zeal, and intelligence, but special faculties born in some few men. The letter of Shadbourne, giving the information about the cattle, is admirable for the purpose intended in matter and manner, and runs as follows:

"Near Blackwater, Sept. 5, 1864.
"General:
"I have just returned from City Point. The defences are as follows:"

Then are given with the greatest precision the points at which troops are stationed, their approximate numbers, where supplies are stored, and the exact distance between the places mentioned.

"At Coggin's Point are 3,000 beeves, attended by 120 men and thirty citizens, without arms. At Sycamore church is one regiment of cavalry (1st District of Columbia). This is the nearest point of the picket line to Coggin's Point (about two miles).

* * * * * *

"The greatest danger, I think, would be on the Jerusalem plank-road in returning.

* * * * * *

"The Tenth corps is on the right (this side Appomattox); Ninth, centre; Fifth, next; Second, on extreme left. I hear that they have a Fifteenth corps, commanded by Ord. From best information Birney commands Tenth corps. This Fifteenth and Sixteenth corps are on the other side of Appomattox. Butler has just returned (yesterday) from convention [he refers to Ben. Butler coming back from a political gathering at the North anent the autumn elections]. It is thought more cavalry is about returning. Colonel ——— is under arrest for drunkenness, I understand—Stratton in command.

" Your obedient scout,

"SHADBOURNE."

The risks run by the scouts in collecting information were of course numerous, but there was no doubt a great fascination in the freedom of the life and the adventures. There were other compensations, too. Picket duty and drudgeries were avoided, and then they were not confined to army rations—scant corn meal and scanter bacon—and though the land was very far from flowing in milk and honey, they knew where to find what little there was. The line of demarkation between a scout and a spy was sometimes very ill-defined, for as the scouts usually dressed in Federal uniforms which they had captured, they were by strict military law subject to the death-penalty as spies, if taken within the enemy's lines, and they were not without unpleasant experiences of that kind. The following incident happening about this time is an example of some of the awkward scrapes into which they might get

Two Confederate scouts were within the Federal lines pursuing their occupation in the direction of City Point. They were dressed in blue overcoats and trousers, and not distinguishable in appearance from Federals. The locality was one with which they were familiar, and near it, in a secluded spot, was a house well known to them, where lived a poor woman, who would often cook for them a meal and also give valuable information which she picked up. So, on this occasion, they concluded to call at the house for the double purpose mentioned. She was a "truly loyal" woman, according to the belief of the Federals. Having fastened their horses in a place concealed from the observation of anyone happening to pass by, the two scouts walked quietly into the house according to their habit, when, to their surprise, in the kitchen, which served also the purposes of parlor and bed-room, there sat two men in blue uniform waiting for some food being prepared. It was too late to withdraw, so the new-comers spoke to the strangers in a friendly way, and conversation ensued while all were waiting for their meal. "Are they Federals, or Confederates in blue uniform?" The Confederates were thus "thinking hard," and so were the other two men. It was all very friendly in appearance, but each couple were fishing, as best they could, to find out what manner of men the others were. The scouts knew full well if these fellows proved to be Federals they must kill them, or be themselves killed; surrender was not to be thought of, because, among other reasons, they would be liable to be shot as spies. The strangers, if Federals, on the other hand, would quite understand that this was exactly what the two men to whom they were talking would be thinking of, provided they were not friends, and therefore they were equally on the *qui vive*. So they all continued to feel their way and watch each other closely, until the woman announced the meal to be ready, when the four sat down together—two and two—on opposite sides of a rough board-table, and commenced to eat. Presently the woman walked behind the chairs of the strangers to pour out some coffee, and, as she filled their cups, unseen by them, gave a quick, warning glance across the table at the scouts. It was only a look, but it was quite enough. In the fraction of a second two revolvers were pointed across the table, and the quick flashes blackened the faces and singed the beards of the poor fellows opposite as the bullets crushed through their heads. It was a ghastly business afterwards, for it was necessary to drag the bodies out and bury them behind an outhouse, where they would not be discovered, and thus bring the poor woman to trouble.

There were two little boys, of ten or eleven years of age, who were said to be among the best scouts, or spies, in the army. When the hostile lines confronted each other closely at Petersburg, these urchins would come over every morning, ostensibly as newsboys, with Petersburg and Richmond papers. They were allowed to do this on signal, for the sake of obtaining the news, but they ran great risk from chance bullets and shells in going to and fro and through the trenches, where the men were, seeking customers. The pluck they showed makes that of a grown man seem small by comparison. They would keep their eyes and ears open, wandering around unnoticed in all sorts of places, as boys will, and thus picked up very valuable information. After awhile they were suspected, but nothing could be absolutely proved against them at that time, and, besides, even a Ben. Butler could hardly have found it in his heart to be very hard on such children, but they were the subject of not a little correspondence at headquarters.

The confidence which the regular scouts had in their ability to penetrate with impunity within the enemy's lines was wonderful. Their chief object was the obtaining of information, but they procured much besides this. If one happened to have an acquaintance among them, and provided the gold or greenbacks for such a commission, he would find little difficulty in securing the equivalent in riding-boots or some other coveted article not purchasable within the Confederacy Fredericksburg was a favorite place for such "shopping," as well as other towns much further north. City Point, too, was a "market," although it was Federal headquarters. No doubt many a "loyal" sutler and attaché of the quartermaster department there increased his income by such trading with anyone who would pay his prices, and was careful not to ask troublesome questions about the ultimate destination of the goods. Indeed, there were regular "underground" arrangements of this kind, worked on "purely business principles," and in these circumstances the purchaser would not be compelled to run much risk. The probability is, that the ramifications of these arrangements extended, for "shopping" and other quite different purposes, very much farther beyond the military lines than most people imagine, and would explain some things happening in those days that have been mysterious to all except a few.

CHAPTER X.

ROSSER AND THE "LAUREL BRIGADE" DETACHED—THE FIGHTING SOUTH OF THE JAMES DURING THE LAST DAYS OF SEPTEMBER—BATTLE OF BURGESS MILL, OCTOBER 27TH—FIVE FORKS AND LEE'S LETTER TO HAMPTON ABOUT THE RESULT.

LATE in September, Rosser's brigade was detached and ordered to the Shenandoah Valley, leaving the cavalry corps on September 27th. It was a parting of comrades tried and true. Their friendship, formed among common dangers and privations, was welded into brotherhood during the terrible month of daily fighting from the Wilderness to Cold Harbor. They parted with the old division never again to meet as soldiers on this side of the Great River on whose bank the few survivors are all now halted: halted, but not for long, and may they all cross in as good style as did the gallant Rosser and his " Laural brigade" when on that September night of '64 they rode over the Blackwater to beard the lion in his den at City Point.

Pursuing the purpose of relating only some of the marked events of the campaign, we pass over the daily skirmishing and picketing and come to the last days of September. At that time General Grant simultaneously renewed his operations to the north and the south of the James river. His principal object was to endeavor to push towards the left for the Southside railroad, hoping to gain ground in that direction, and then on the north side there was a possibility to surprise Richmond, or, at all events, a chance to make a diversion there. Such are the advantages of always having at one's disposal three or four soldiers to every one on the other side. Moreover, it was necessary for political reasons to appear to be doing something, for at that period there was a deadly, weary feeling creeping over the North about the war. The premium on gold, the thermometer of public feeling, was going up by leaps and bounds. People were becoming shy of the "attrition" process. *"Dulce et decorum est,"* etc., but then there is a limit to sentiment. Correspondence between Grant and the Federal authorities shows great misgivings about the enforcement of the conscription, and also as to the quality of the new recruits being received, and keen dissatisfaction with the course of the Governor of Massachusetts and officials of some other States in buying cheap Southern negroes, as Grant expressed it, to fill their quotas. So a movement on both sides of the river must be made. On the north side General Grant had Ben. Butler in command, probably the most incompetent of any of the "political generals" on either side, and that is saying

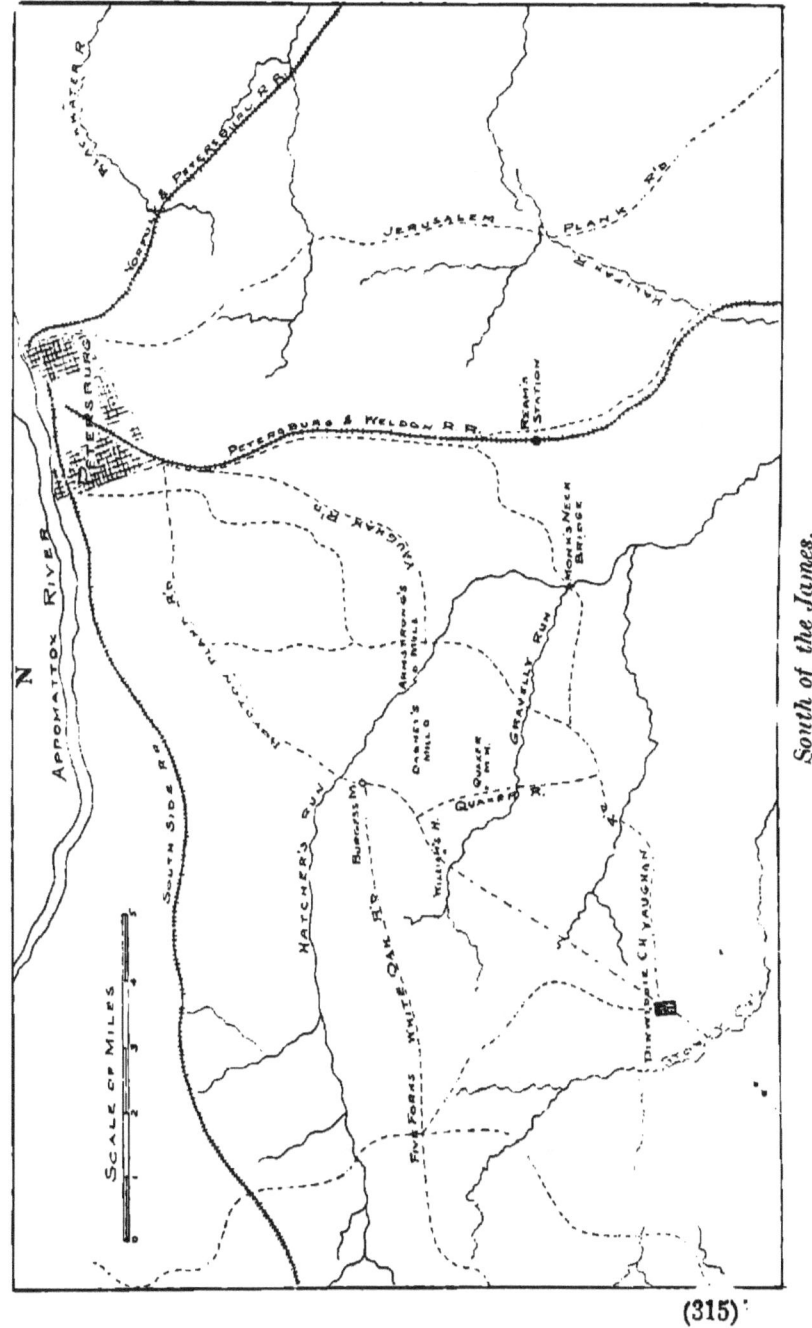

South of the James.

very much. To his enemies Butler was cruel, but for his friends he was worse, imbecile in a military sense, and no doubt to no one was he such a nuisance as to General Grant, who deserves no little credit for tolerating him for policy, and at the same time practically shooting over his head. If countless orders, proclamations, and despatches fulminated from a safe distance in the rear could destroy fortifications and troops, there would not have been an earth-work standing or a soldier alive between the Potomac and the Rio Grande. So Ben. Butler commenced the movement with a general order of a kindergarten nature, several pages in length, explaining exactly how Richmond was to be taken, what was to be done after they got there, and promising double pay for six months to the men and promotion to officers of regiments, brigades, or divisions arriving there first, except to major-generals, to whom, as he considerately explains, no special bribe need be given to induce them to perform their duty, which was a back-handed compliment to the others, and disgusted them very much. However, a hare must needs be caught before it is cooked, and therefore we will concern ourselves no more about Ben. Butler's peculiar modes of warfare, for on the south side of the river real " business " is meant, for there are Meade, Hancock, and Warren, as well as Grant.

On September 27th M. C. Butler's division on the Vaughn road, west of the Weldon railroad, was attacked, but the enemy was driven back and the lines re-established and some prisoners taken. On the following day the enemy poured a strong force of infantry into the trenches temporarily occupied by Dearing's brigade, and captured the works. One of those incidents happened there which illustrates the strong individuality of the men. A private in Graham's battery of horse artillery was with his gun in a small work, which was carried by the enemy. As they flocked in they shouted to him to "surrender!" to which he paid no attention, but managed to get horses attached to the gun, and mounting one of the wheelers, commenced to move out. An officer rushed forward and attempted to run him through with his sword, but the artilleryman, armed only with a stick he had caught up, felled him to the ground, whipped up his horses, which the Federals endeavored to stop with bayonet thrusts, and clattered away in safety. The poor horses only were wounded. To an artilleryman the gun he has helped to handle in a hundred fights is as dear as his own child.

After consultation with General Heth it was determined to attack the enemy in the position he had attained, the infantry to strike in front, and Hampton on the left flank. In pursuance of this plan the cavalry were moved to a suitable location, and meantime the infantry on both sides became engaged. The enemy proceeded to bring up reinforcements, and in doing this exposed their left flank, which movement was quickly taken advantage of by Hampton, who threw a force upon them, gallantly led by General W H. F Lee in person. The men dismounted, went forward in line of battle, firing no shots until within close range, and then pouring it in regularly, and advancing all the while. The enemy at this point was completely routed, and many cut off. About nine hundred prisoners and ten flags were captured in this fight. McGregor with his horse artillery kept up with the line of battle in magnificent style, continuously firing, as he went forward, with great effect. It was a well-conducted and brilliant affair, and important, as it checked the further advance of the Federals in these movements south of the James, although it did not wrest from them the ground already gained. The "Army and Navy Gazette," of October 8, 1864, speaking of this engagement, says, showing what was thought at the time :

"Whatever the objects of the demonstrations, they have evidently not yet attained success. The 'thin line' which we are told that Warren found on the left on Friday appears to have been rapidly augmented. At all events the flanking column, which burst in between two divisions of our troops and swept off so many men, shows the enemy to have been in anything but desperate straits. To this new disaster (which resembles some previous ones on similar occasions) the check in the present phase of the campaign is due."

On the next day, there was a considerable amount of successful fighting by the cavalry with the enemy's infantry and cavalry. It was deeply to be regretted, however, that in one of these charges General Dunovant went down, gallantly leading Butler's old brigade. As he fell, his foot caught in the stirrup and the **body** was dragged until the saddle turned and thus released the foot, but he was then quite dead. Dr. Fontaine, the medical director of the corps, hearing that he was wounded, galloped to the front to render prompt assistance, and had nearly reached him on the errand of mercy when, by the explosion of a shell, he himself was mortally wounded. Surely no man ever met a grander death, for he died for his fellow-man. Fontaine was very able professionally, but, more than that, he was a true man. On one occasion, some two or three so-called assistant surgeons (evaders of military service under this disguise) at a field hospital, became drunk, and one of them in particular was very insolent to wounded privates. Shortly afterwards Fontaine arrived, and one indignant private informed him of the occurrence and requested redress. He investigated the matter at once, ordered the drunken offenders under arrest, and they were subsequently put into the ranks of the infantry. General Lee in a letter to General Hampton writes:

"I grieve with you at the loss of General Dunovant and Dr. Fontaine—two officers whom it will be difficult to replace."

This closed the serious fighting in this movement, the Federals having been unsuccessful in making further material progress in the direction of the Southside railroad, but holding what ground they had obtained.

After the termination of the operations just referred to, the cavalry was engaged in no important encounters until October 27th, though, in the meantime, there was much desultory skirmishing. The event occuring on October 27th, which is usually termed the battle of Burgess Mill, I propose to relate in some detail, because it was an important affair, and proved to be the last very serious attempt made by Grant during the campaign of 1864 to turn Lee's right flank and seize the Southside railroad, to compel the evacuation of Petersburg. There is another reason, also, for dwelling more at length on this engagement, because the main features of this unsuccessful attempt are the same as those of the movement, five months later at Five Forks, which had a very different result.

This battle was deliberately planned beforehand, and was a sequence of preceding movements, and was specifically stated to be an attempt to seize the Southside railroad. As the Petersburg fortifications could not be taken by approaches nor assault, and Ben. Butler could produce no effect on Richmond on the north side of the river, there was no alternative but to extend the Federal lines round to the left (west) until a permanent lodgment could be made on the Southside railroad, and, if this could be effected, Petersburg and, as a consequence, Richmond would no longer be tenable. It required no military sagacity to perceive this, but the difficulty was to effect it, for Lee stubbornly barred the way.

General Grant, during September, had been urging Stanton to send him at least forty thousand more recruits for his Virginia armies, and these had been gradually received. They came from all races and climes—from the woolly-headed African to the German with flaxen locks. By November bad weather and bad roads might increase the difficulty of forward movements. Moreover, on November 5th would occur the Presidential and Congressional elections at the North, which would determine whether the existing or a different political and military policy would be pursued. The masses were heartily tired of the war, and almost every one was dissatisfied with the lack of visible success in the military operations. It would be very desirable, therefore, to gain a great victory, because of its favorable effect on the elections, and even an important movement, if not a crushing disaster, could be represented as a victory, and would be better than inaction. So, for every reason, the commanding general was urged to fight before November, and to fight he therefore determined.

Preparations for the contemplated action having been made, orders were issued to portions of the command to move out by half-past two A. M. on October 27th, and other bodies were to march at later hours, depending upon their position, so that the advance would encounter their enemy at the desired point by the first daylight. All the force that could be possibly spared from the fortifications was ordered out. In fact, there was some raking and scraping done, though one would think that without this the numbers were all-sufficient. The forces consisted of all of the Second, Fifth, and Ninth corps not left in the trenches, and Gregg's division of cavalry, the latter numbering five thousand four hundred and seventy-one strong after the battle, making the total force about forty thousand men. They were provided with four days' rations, showing the intention to hold what it was hoped to gain. Ben. Butler at the same time was ordered to make a strong diversion on the north side of the river to draw troops from Lee, which he proceeded to do with his customary fuss, anticipating as usual the capture of Richmond.

The Federal force executed well the movement out, and proceeded to follow the orders given. The Second (Hancock's) corps occupied the left, marching down the Vaughn road to Hatcher's run, the extreme right of the Confederate line, and in connection with this corps was Gregg's cavalry division. Their task was to turn and extend round Lee's right, which, successfully executed and held, meant the seizing of the Southside railroad, and, consequently, the enforced evacuation of Petersburg and Richmond. This is easily understood by a glance at a map. The movement would, if consummated, have been an anticipation of Five Forks. The other two corps were on the right of Hancock's, and confronted more or less fortified parts of the Confederate line. These latter accomplished nothing of any consequence, and were not heavily engaged. It is only therefore with Hancock's corps and the cavalry of Gregg that we are much interested.

Grant's plan of attack was based on the belief that Lee's extreme right, on Hatcher's run, was not fortified strongly, in which he was correctly informed. The difficulty with Lee was to extend his line so far with the comparatively small force he had. His was "the slender line of gray." But Grant was not correct as to the strength of the lines which his corps on the right were to attack, as was demonstrated to him by the result.

By daylight on the morning of the 27th Hampton's pickets were driven in all along his line, from Armstrong's mill, on Hatcher's run, to Monck's Neck bridge, on his extreme right, a distance of about two miles. It was promptly done, and the camps behind were obliged to get into saddle without attending to the niceties of the toilette, or to breakfast, which was postponed by unanimous consent until about eight o'clock that evening. Some dismounted men, who were in camp, always as wretched as fish out of water, were forced, much against their will, to move in undignified haste, swearing like orthodox troopers, amid much pleasant chaff from their more fortunate comrades on horseback. Hancock's infantry crossed Hatcher's run at the Vaughn road and Armstrong's mill, and Gregg's cavalry at Monck's Neck bridge, two miles farther south, at the junction of Hatcher's run and Gravely's run. Butler reinforced his pickets and soon became quite heavily engaged with the infantry advancing towards the Boydton plank-road and the Quaker road. Meantime, Hampton apprehended that if the gap between Butler's left and Hatcher's run was not filled, the Federal infantry would proceed up the run towards Burgess mill, two and a half miles farther up, where the Boydton plank-road crosses that stream. He therefore sent Venable, of his staff, to order Dearing's brigade, then in the works on the north side of the run, to fill up this gap. General A. P Hill, commanding, did not think Dearing's brigade could well be spared from the works, and sent back a message to Hampton to that effect by Venable, but on returning, the latter was captured by the enemy, and therefore Hampton did not receive this communication, and remained under the impression that Dearing's brigade would fill the gap. This left the way open along the run to the crossing by the Boydton road, and Hancock accordingly proceeded up the stream to that point and attacked there. Meantime, finding that the enemy

(331)

was advancing from the Vaughn road down the Quaker road towards its junction with the Boydton road near the run, Hampton took position at the Quaker meeting-house and checked him, and General W H. F Lee was ordered to move up the Military road so as to strike him in the rear. But at this juncture it was discovered that Hancock had passed up the gap mentioned, to the Boydton road, thus getting in Hampton's rear, and his cavalry was perceived going down the White Oak road, which leads to Five Forks, distant somewhat less than five miles from the Boydton road. To counteract this, Butler, withdrawing from the Quaker meeting-house, faced about and went galloping over to the White Oak road to check the advance in that direction, a small portion of his force being left to engage the enemy on the Boydton road near Wilson's. The Federals were encountered on the White Oak road and stopped, Butler's line extending on both sides of the road with its left on Burgess mill-pond. W H. F Lee was ordered to bring his division to the Boydton road and attack there, which he did with great spirit. Up to this time, about four o'clock P M., the cavalry alone was covering the right flank of the army from Hancock's infantry and Gregg's cavalry. Now General Heth, of Hill's command, was communicated with, and it was decided to cross the infantry over the run and make an attack in concert with Hampton. As soon as the musketry announced the infantry engaged, Butler charged, with his whole line dismounted, across an open field and drove the enemy rapidly towards the Boydton road. Simultaneously W H. F Lee advanced down the Boydton road, his left uniting with Butler's right. The enemy was enveloped on three sides from a point on the Quaker road to Burgess mill-pond. Hancock was thus driven from his position on the roads and became massed in the fields east of the Boydton road, isolated from the support of the other corps, defeated. Lee's right flank was covered. As Butler's division swept forward to connect their right with W H. F Lee's left, Hampton being individually in the front, Lieutenant William Preston Hampton, A. D. C. to his father, the General, was mortally wounded while gallantly charging with the division and cheering on the men, and his brother, Lieutenant Wade Hampton, temporarily attached to the General's staff, was also disabled. Lieutenant-Colonel Jeffords also was killed when conspicuously at the head of his regiment, Fifth South Carolina, and Major Barker, A. A. G. of Butler's division, who at once took his place, quickly fell, wounded.

The writer regrets that in describing these movements it is necessary to introduce to the reader so many names of localities and roads which may not be familiar to him, and of themselves are dry details. This, however, is unavoidable, if the true development of the battle is to be properly understood. The sketch-map of the topography, attached, will make the evolutions sufficiently clear at a glance. South of Hatcher's run the right flank of the army was, on that day up to about four o'clock P M., protected only by the Confederate cavalry from the Federal infantry and cavalry, as has been already stated. The importance of this need not be dwelt upon, for it is self-evident that the turning of this flank and a lodgment meant the gravest disaster, if not ruin. North of Hatcher's run, Dearing's brigade, dismounted in the trenches, and other dismounted cavalry, assisted the infantry to hold the works. In the attack, delivered at about four o'clock P M., the cavalry, as has been shown, had their full share, in conjunction with Heth's infantry, in finally defeating Hancock. All of the fighting this day, of any importance, done by the cavalry, was performed dismounted, as infantry. In this engagement the principal features of the Federal movements, and the resulting necessity of interposing between them and the strategical points covering or commanding the right flank of the Army of Northern Virginia, are so similar to those of Five Forks as to furnish an interesting comparison in many respects. They give to the battle of Burgess Mill a special meaning, viewed in the vivid light of the tragic memories of Five Forks.

The complete success of the charge last described relieved Mahone, on the north side of the run, from the fire of Hancock, to which, before this, he had been exposed, as well as to attack from the other side by the corps manœuvring on Hancock's right, which was divided from the latter during the battle by a wide interval. Why this separation of these two corps, intended to act in concert, had been permitted, was matter of controversy for a long time between the commanders concerned, but that is a "family quarrel." It probably occurred through confusion in manœuvring through ground of a very rough character, broken up by dense thickets, swampy places, and small runs. Troops will naturally in such places experience great risks of confusion and missing of direction, especially if they are under fire at the time. We now see, from the published despatches and reports on the Federal side, that the withdrawal of Butler's division from contact with Hancock's corps on the Quaker road, for the purpose of cutting off the troops on the White Oak road, was very naturally misunderstood by Hancock and Meade. It was believed by them to have been a repulse of infantry effected. The long Enfields of Butler's command frequently misled the enemy as to the character of the troops. And then when, after its mission in regard to the force on the White Oak road had been accomplished, Butler's division rushed in upon Hancock, this appearance of "troops coming out of the woods" on his flank and rear, as the Federal commander expressed it, was supposed to be a new attack of fresh infantry. The success of this charge convinced Hancock of his inability to place himself in rear of the Confederate lines, or to make and maintain connection with the Federal corps operating on his right. He therefore decided to retreat lest he should be entirely cut off the next day. This withdrawal was accordingly commenced soon after dark, the dead and badly wounded being left behind. Hampton's last movement had been completed just as a dark night set in, accompanied by a cold autumn rain. This prevented observation of the enemy's retreat. Meantime the Confederate cavalry line was maintained in its position with the intention of resuming the attack in the morning. Mounted videttes were thrown out and the dismounted men rested where they were, and took the exceedingly frugal breakfast which had been postponed from the morning. It was not, in fact, a very agreeable meal, in spite of hunger, for the fighting having gone on until darkness settled down, the dead and many of the wounded necessarily remained where they fell, and the consciousness of the presence of sufferers, almost within touch, did not furnish an appetizing sauce for the much-needed food. Some non-combatants hold the theory, that wounded men left in the rain experience relief by the coolness and moisture, but, believe me, this is a fallacy. The nervous system being to a greater or less extent prostrated from lack of food and deprivation of coffee, tea, or other stimulant, and the strength sapped by over-exertion, loss of blood, and suffering, there ensues a terrible physical chilliness, which creeps over you as the pitiless rain comes down, and you feel lonely, and abandoned by God and man, and dispute the wisdom of the scheme of creation by which it happened you were ever born. When assistance would at length come, all relief practicable was afforded, but that was too often little enough. The avowed system pursued by the Federal authorities was to capture or destroy, wherever found, and to exclude by blockade and as contraband of war, all surgical instruments, medicines, and hospital supplies pertaining to the Confederates, which was done for the purpose of increasing the mortality among their wounded and sick. This, and the non-exchange of prisoners of war, were parts of the "attrition" process.

Throughout the day of battle, and especially on the plank-road, Chew's artillery did splendid execution. Hart's battery suffered severely in casualties, but kept up its good work to the end. Here, Captain Hart lost his leg, but had at least the comfort of knowing the sacrifice was made in no petty skirmish, but in an important victory. This battery was, during the four consecutive years of the war, under fire—counting skirmishes and battles—on one hundred and forty-three distinct occasions. This statement is founded not on guess-work, but actual data. It has been asserted on good military authority that no other battery ever had such a record made during four consecutive years. A fair comprehension of what manner of men composed it may be gained by reading "The Burial of the Guns," by Nelson Page.

During this fight privates in Butler's division fired over eighty rounds from their Enfield muzzle-loaders. They shot, not in volleys, but at will, and the next morning in going over the ground opposite to them it was seen they had not wasted their ammunition, for in some places the corpses were thickly strewn. The losses of the cavalry, however, in killed and wounded were very light in proportion to the fire sustained, and of prisoners they had almost none taken, but captured 239. The enemy's losses are set down in their official returns as 1,902, but, as previously remarked, returns do not always agree, for 1,365 prisoners were delivered in Richmond, and these were in addition to the killed and wounded, which were numerous. The Federal infantry, as a rule, shot very wildly, many of them no doubt being new recruits. Twigs and small branches cut down by bullets would be seen falling from the trees from a height of thirty to sixty feet or more from the ground. Some prisoners taken were unable to understand a word spoken to them until addressed in German. A man, one of the many red-haired descendants of the ancient Irish kings, whose "be Jabers" is so familiar to our ears, was found next morning kneeling against a tree, apparently in the very act of firing his rifle, which was full-cocked at his shoulder. Turning to look more closely, it was discovered he was stiff and stark. Death must have been instantaneous, but the strange thing is, that his body, instead of being convulsed by the last struggle, should have been, as it were, petrified in its final attitude, like a dog on the point. One other exactly similar case was noticed on another occasion after a battle, and that fellow, too, was an Irishman.

Mention has been made that Preston Hampton fell mortally wounded while leading with distinguished gallantry in the last charge. He was a most lovable boy in disposition, gentle and attractive in manner, generous in word and deed, manly and strong in physique, and brave to a fault; sure to be dearly loved by a parent, and to have a very warm place in the hearts of comrades. Leaving college when only seventeen years of age, he had joined the first troops called for by his State, and was present at the reduction of Fort Sumter. Immediately after that he joined, as private, one of the cavalry companies of the Hampton Legion and went with that command to Virginia. Afterwards he was detailed as orderly at headquarters, and thus saw the service performed by the infantry of the Legion, including the battle of Seven Pines and the "Seven Days' Battles Around Richmond." On his father's transfer to the cavalry he accompanied him, and was in all the fights in which the brigade was engaged. After a time he was appointed aide-de-camp on General Hampton's staff, where he served continuously until his death. He showed not only brilliant daring, but also the nerve and cool judgment in danger that mark the true soldier. He had been wounded on two previous occasions, and on others had had horses shot under him, and now he was to meet his death in the full flush of victory in one of the finest charges of the war. His father, always in the front, had been near at hand when his son fell from his horse, and for a moment dismounted, and, bending down over the dying boy, tenderly kissed his forehead, and then gently whispered to him some words not heard by others amidst the din of battle. After hastily giving directions for his removal, together with his other son, who was also wounded, but not so seriously, he remounted and rode forward with the advancing line. Such was a commander's duty, but it was a hard one to perform.

It seems from correspondence to which there is now access that General Grant, in company with Meade, crossed the run during the day and rode down to near where Hancock was engaged. Meade afterwards remarks, in a communication to Grant, that if they had proceeded farther on a certain road referred to, they would have come, as it turned out, upon the enemy. They little knew the danger they were encountering, for the opposing lines were so frequently changed in position during different times that day—what was the front or flank at one period being the rear at another, or *vice versa*—that it would not have been

Father and son.

strange if they in their wanderings had been picked up as prisoners, and in this case the history of our planet, at least of this part of it, might have been very different. General Grant returned to City Point in the evening. That firm face was grave and anxious, as he smoked his cigar, we may be sure. How much longer would his murmuring people endure the losses? What if Hancock's list of dead and wounded reaches ten or fifteen thousand to-day, and the voters of the North next month elect McClellan as President? How much longer will the thread suspending the sword over his head sustain this continued "attrition?"

The Federals, as has been stated, retreated during the night. In the morning they were pursued by the cavalry and harassed until they reached their fortifications. They left behind them, besides dead and wounded, several caissons and many small arms and accoutrements.

Lest there should be any misapprehension of

facts, we will quote here portions of a correspondence between General Lee and General Hampton, which explains itself.

On October 29, 1864, General Hampton wrote to General Lee as follows:

> "A paragraph in your official report leads me to suppose that you are under a misapprehension in reference to the movements of the enemy on 27th inst. Your report says that 'the enemy crossed Rowanty creek below Burgess mill and forced back the cavalry in the afternoon.' To correct this misapprehension I will give a brief statement of what occurred in anticipation of my report."

Then follows an account of the movement, the same in effect as that contained in his official report. General Lee replies on October 31, 1864:

"I have received your letter of 29th inst., recounting the movements of the enemy on the 27th.

"My report to the Secretary of War was formed from the telegraphic despatch from General Hill. From the lines you quote I perceive there is an error in punctuation. The stop should have been after 'cavalry.' I intended by the use of the latter word to designate only that portion as being driven back which was opposed to the advance of the enemy at the creek, but I did not wish to particularize, as I did not desire the enemy to know what force was on our extreme right.

*　　*　　*　　*　　*　　*

"In a letter to General Hill to-day, I expressed my gratification at the conduct of the troops in general, and of the cavalry in particular, desiring him to communicate my thanks to you and your command."

As it throws light upon the dispositions

during the engagement of October 27th, and also upon the nature of the defences on the extreme right of the Confederates at a later date, we will now quote the following extract from a letter of October 24, 1864, to General Lee from General Hampton

"There have been no operations of my command lately which required a report, and I have been engaged in assisting the infantry in completing a new line of works, which extends to Hatcher's run. This work is now finished, and the disposition of my troops is as follows: Seven hundred men are in the trenches, their right resting on the creek, about one and a half miles above Armstrong's mill. Butler occupies the line from the latter point to Monck's Neck bridge, and Lee extends to the Halifax road. I have erected five dams in the creek, covering them with works on the south bank. These works and the dams will render this line very secure. Dearing is at Burgess mill, and he has orders, in case the enemy advances, to place his whole command at once in the trenches on the right of the infantry. To-day General Hill rode over the lines with me, and I proposed to him that he should hold them to the creek with his infantry and artillery If he can do this, and he says that he can if he can get one thousand or one thousand five hundred more men, I propose to place all my dismounted men, about eight hundred, on the south bank of the creek, holding that line. The cavalry can then all be concentrated in supporting distance, and, if the enemy attacks, I can throw a force of from three to four thousand men on his flank by crossing at one of my dams, keeping at the same time sufficient mounted troops to check any advance of the Federal cavalry

"If you can give General Hill men enough to return mine now in the trenches, so as to enable me to carry out the plan suggested, I think that you need feel no uneasiness as to an attack on my right.

"I have examined all the ground and feel sanguine of the success of such a movement as I have indicated. My command is growing stronger every day, and it is in good condition for a fight. Butler received two hundred and seventy-five horses to-day, and Lee can mount two thousand five hundred men. If my command can be concentrated I shall be able to take upwards of five thousand men into action. We are using every effort not only to strengthen our line, but to augment our numbers."

To this letter General Lee replied under date of October 26th, the day before the battle of Burgess Mill, as follows:

"Your letter of the 24th is received. I am much pleased to hear of the improvement and increase of your command, and of your confidence in the strength of your position. It would afford me great gratification if I could give General Hill the additional infantry to enable him to return your troops, as you propose, as I can see that much benefit would result from it. But the difficulty is to get the men. I have written to him to say that the only source we have to depend upon is the conscription now going on. I hope he will be considerably strengthened by this means, and I have requested him to co-operate in your proposition to the extent of his ability."

On the following day the attack provided against by Hampton occurred, and, as has been seen from General Lee's letter, the additional 1,000 to 1,500 troops desired could not be furnished to General Hill. It will also be noted that notwithstanding the inability to obtain this augmentation of the force the battle was decisively won.

Ben. Butler, of course, accomplished nothing beyond much fussing on the north side of the James on October 27th, and the expedition carefully prepared, with a large force, to turn Lee's right was completely defeated, as we have seen. A better showing for the affair was attempted by the Federals at the North for the sake of the November elections, but it fell flat, as the facts were too patent; the purpose of the attack had been avowed beforehand and was admitted in the official despatches, and it was clear to all that this purpose had not been attained, for the three corps and their cavalry returned to their starting point. Some of the northern newspapers ventilated the matter pretty thoroughly. Of course they got most of the details wrong, but the main thing, the result, they could hardly miss. Two of the principal New York papers published accounts deemed particularly unjust to some of the higher officers concerned. War Secretary Stanton wished to have the correspondents in camp of these newspapers punished by court-martial, asserting that although citizens and not enlisted men they were subject to military law, and he intended to have them brought to Washington to be punished by a military commission. The offence, however, if any there was, had been committed by the editors through publication in New York, and not within the lines of the army. General Hancock was one of the officers thought to be unfairly represented by these correspondents, and he wished them merely sent out of camp, but, being a just and generous gentleman as well as a fine soldier, he would have nothing to do with the proceedings proposed, which he considered equally repugnant to fair play and to the laws of the land, and so Stanton dropped the matter.

After the battle of Burgess Mill, there was no serious attempt made during that campaign by the Federal army to turn Lee's right flank, and thus gain possession of the Southside railroad. About five months later occurred the battle of Five Forks, which is not a part of this narrative, dealing only with the campaign of 1864. But a resemblance exists, except in result, between Burgess Mill and Five Forks which challenges attention, as we have already said. The story of the latter is too well known to require repetition here. At that time General Hampton was in North Carolina commanding the cavalry with Johnston's army, and with him was Butler's division. The cavalry corps of the Army of Northern Virginia had consisted, in the autumn, of two divisions, Butler's and W H. F Lee's, and in the following spring was composed of the last-named division, together with those of Fitz. Lee and Rosser, the latter having been made a major-general and assigned to a division while in the Shenandoah Valley, and a better officer there was not in the army. These three divisions, commanded by

Fitzhugh Lee as senior major-general, numbered about 7,000 men, which was nearly one-third more than had been available during the previous autumn. Opposed to them were three divisions of Federal cavalry under Sheridan, aggregating 13,209 "present for duty" by the report of March 31, 1865. The disparity in numbers of about two to one in favor of the Federals was not necessarily daunting to the cavalry of the Army of Northern Virginia, for against equal and greater odds they had won many victories. The odds against Hampton at Trevilian, it will be remembered, were as two compared with one, and yet he beat his opponent in that cavalry duel, prevented him from accomplishing any of the purposes for which the expedition had been made, and finally forced him to regain his own army by a long detour. Had it not been for lack of co-operation by one of Hampton's divisions in that fight he would probably have crushed and destroyed

Sheridan's entire force, as was the deliberate purpose of his plan of battle. Five Forks was about a mile south of the nearest part of Hatcher's run and some four miles north and slightly west of Dinwiddie Courthouse, and its occupation by the enemy enabled him to control the Southside railroad, which compelled the evacuation of Petersburg. Every one knows that these results were effected by the Federals, and that the immediate withdrawal from Richmond was a necessary consequence. The Confederates at the battle of Five Forks faced nearly in the direction of Dinwiddie, with Pickett's infantry in the centre, all of the cavalry on the right, except one division, which was held in reserve on the other side (north) of Hatcher's run. The enemy's infantry (Warren) came up the run (westerly) unobserved, turned Pickett's flank, and, getting in his rear, doubled him up. If this position had been held, Lee's lines would have been intact, and he could have withdrawn from Petersburg quietly and formed a junction with Johnston's army, if he deemed it advisable to do so, or proceeded to more easily defensible positions elsewhere. Of very great interest in this connection is the following letter from General Lee to General Hampton, written four months after the end of the war:

"NEAR CARTERSVILLE, August 1, 1865.
My Dear General:

"I was very much gratified at the reception of your letter of the 5th ultimo. I have been very anxious concerning you, and could obtain no satisfactory information. * * * You cannot regret as much as I did, that you were not with us at our final struggle. The absence of the troops which I had sent to North and South Carolina, was I believe, the cause of our immediate disaster. Our small force of cavalry [a large portion of the men who had been sent to the interior to winter their horses had not rejoined their regiments] was unable to resist the united cavalry under Sheridan, which obliged me to detach Pickett's division to Fitz. Lee's support, thereby weakening my main line, and yet not accomplishing my purpose. If you had been there with all of our cavalry, the result at Five Forks would have been different. But how long the contest could have been prolonged, it is difficult to say. It is over, and though the present is depressing and disheartening, I trust the future may prove brighter We must at least hope so, and each one do his part to make it so. * * * That every happiness may attend you and yours is the earnest prayer of

Your friend,

R. E. Lee."

The parts of this letter omitted, indicated in the above by stars, are concerning matters which have no reference to the subjects spoken of in the quoted portion.

The statement made by Lee, from whose ruling there is no appeal, is explicit: " If you had been there with all of our cavalry, the result at Five Forks would have been different."

As for the *morale* of the Confederate troops of all arms at this period, it was excellent in spite of all theories of exhaustion now in vogue to the contrary. Even after the disaster at Five Forks, the significance of which was as well understood by privates as by generals, the temper of the army remained firm and courageous. All the evidence of eye-witnesses proves that the troops marched forth from Petersburg in high heart and absolute confidence that " Marse Robert will bring it out all right." Indeed, the release from the terrible confinement of the trenches produced an elation of spirits. The freshness of spring, the green fields, and budding trees and flowers, were in blessed contrast to the squalor and wretchedness which they had been enduring all those weary months and were now leaving behind. And Lee, too, felt the influence of all this. It was said by all that he never looked more inspiring, grander, or nobler than when, without thought of surrender, he rode at the head of those columns which would submit to no defeat. It was not until the army, bearing up with uncomplaining pluck against hunger, reached Amelia Courthouse, where ample rations had been ordered to be provided, that Lee's face, for the first and last time ever known, became for a moment ghastly pale. For the traitors, or imbeciles of a department always the worst, had failed to obey orders, although the means of doing so were in their hands, and no food was available. By that crime, through starvation, not by arms and numbers, was the fate of the Army of Northern Virginia sealed. Otherwise they could still have gained the slopes of the

Blue Ridge, and behind those impregnable ramparts constructed by the Almighty, have maintained their organization and prestige intact, and become daily stronger in numbers from recruits. That such a movement should have been made months before this, was General Lee's decided opinion, as is now well known, but it was overruled by the Richmond authorities for political reasons. At an earlier period such a withdrawal could have been easily effected and the war prolonged indefinitely This was Lee's opinion. He said even at the last: "With my army in the mountains of Virginia, I could carry on this war for twenty years longer" This may at some time prove an opinion worth remembering, if in the future foreign wars in which we shall be involved our coast cities should be seized by hostile fleets, or armies of overpowering strength. Loud clamors would then no doubt arise from the timid for peace at any price, coming, perhaps, from the same mouths noisiest in cheers for easily gained victories over weak foes. But in spite of all vociferations to the contrary, we can still maintain ourselves by force of arms, if we are willing to endure privations, to fight stoutly under good discipline, to die, if our turn comes, among the inland fastnesses which the rivers and mountains of our land have provided. As early as October 4, 1864, General Lee wrote to Mr. Seddon, Secretary of War, as follows

"I beg leave to inquire whether there is any prospect of my obtaining any increase to this army. If not, it will be very difficult for us to maintain ourselves. The enemy's numerical superiority enables him to hold his lines with an adequate force, and extend on each flank with numbers so much greater than ours, that we can only meet his corps, increased by recent recruits, with a division reduced by long and arduous service. We cannot fight to advantage with such odds, and there is the gravest reason to apprehend the result of every encounter."

If this warning had been heeded, a timely withdrawal could have been effected.

CHAPTER XI.

CAMP CORRESPONDENCE—STONY CREEK—MILES TRIES TO ATTACK THE RIGHT FLANK—WARREN'S RAID ON THE WELDON RAILROAD—END OF THE CAMPAIGN OF '64—HAMPTON ORDERED TO SOUTH CAROLINA—MORALE OF BUTLER'S DIVISION—CAPTURE OF KILPATRICK'S CAMP—THE LONE DAMSEL—BUTLER'S CHARGE—"BUCKLAND RACES"—THE CHALLENGE.

NOVEMBER came in quietly, almost peacefully, for the cavalry, the only interruption being the inevitable picketing and petty skirmishes. On the north side of the James, Ben. Butler no longer let loose and whistled up his trusty dogs of war for an original, duly patented *coup de main* on Richmond. By Stanton's selection he was appointed for the time being election standard-bearer, and headed a column of some ten thousand soldiers of all arms ("preferably Western troops," as General Grant recommended), and northward, not southward, they marched, the objective point New York, there to see to the election to be held on November 5th, a sort of mission which was to his taste, and well accomplished.

On the south side of the river Gregg's cavalry were inactive. The commanding general said they were too weak in numbers to attempt enterprises of moment, but by the November returns of "men present for duty," this division alone was credited with 6,189 sabres, more than Hampton's entire force.

Later in November, Grant was contemplating an attack on Lee's lines on the right, but thought them too strong. On November 30th he wired Meade that he had just received a copy of a newspaper published in Augusta,

Ga., containing a notice signed "Wade Hampton," instructing his men to rendezvous there, and that he was uncertain whether this meant that General Hampton, with a part of his cavalry, had left Virginia, or whether the signature might not, in fact, represent that of a son of General Hampton. He expressed the opinion that if Hampton had left Virginia, it would be a good time to attack, but not otherwise. A little later their correspondence shows that they had discovered Hampton had not left Virginia, and had heard that Mrs. Hampton was honoring headquarters with her presence, from which they concluded it would not be a favorable moment to attack on the right, the corps probably being in force there. However, they were uneasy at doing nothing, and so determined to send the cavalry reconnoitering south of Reams station towards Stony creek, on the Weldon railroad. Accordingly Gregg, with his division, or the chief part of it, went in that direction, and

Lieutenant Wade Hampton, eldest son of General Hampton, wounded in the battle of Burgess Mill.

(371)

near Stony creek, on December 1st, succeeded in surprising a small number of dismounted (without horses) men, stationed there as guard over a few supplies, and a construction squad. All, or nearly all, the guard were captured, but as only 170 prisoners in all were shown by the Federal return of the raid, it must have been a very trifling affair, and the disproportion of numbers enormous. But the Federals returned to Reams station and a congratulatory order was issued to the troops for this achievement. M. C. Butler, hearing of this raid, started his division to overtake them, but they "had the foot on him," as the countrymen say, and escaped to the cover of the infantry. It was in the middle of the night that Butler's men were routed out of their blankets to get into saddle, and the first very cold night of the winter, so that they did not feel very cheerful about it. But some of them were soon laughing over a funny sight. One very nice fellow had had the misfortune to lose an eye, and had replaced it by one of glass. His habit was each night, before rolling up in his blanket, to remove from the socket and put this false eye in a cup of water by his side. He had done so on this occasion, and when he awoke to mount, he found the water in the cup frozen to the bottom and the glass effectually encased in ice, not to be removed until melted out over a fire. Of course, there was no time then to do this. He was compelled, therefore, to accept the situation, pocket the ice and the eye, and cover the place in his face where it ought to have been with the extemporized expedient of an old stocking, which gave him a most grotesque appearance. He did not "damn his eyes," but swore at the one offending false member in a manner which must have made it wink for shame.

Encouraged by the reconnoissance of Gregg, which seemed to show but small force guarding the Weldon railroad south of Reams station, the Federal commander determined to make an attempt to destroy the Weldon railroad as far south as Hicksford or Bellefield, on the Meherrin river, about twenty miles south of Stony creek. For although he had effected a lodgment at Reams station, thus cutting off there this line of communication with Lee's army, yet the railroad was still of use to the Confederates, as supplies from the South, brought to Stony creek, which place Lee yet held, could be wagoned to the army. So preparations were made by the Federals to send out an expedition for this purpose, consisting of twenty-two thousand infantry, four thousand cavalry, and five batteries, under Warren, to which were added afterwards eight thousand additional troops. At the same time Nelson A. Miles was started out with a heavy column on the Confederate right flank, on Hatcher's run, to try his hand developing the position there, and to ascertain what troops were detached to pursue Warren. If he found it practicable, however, he was to make a diversion in favor of the latter and strike hard. Miles was told, too, to feel his way cautiously, and to "look out" he was not cut off, and these latter orders he closely complied with and made no vigorous movements. He confronted the works at the run, and there was a little, more or less harmless, skirmishing, but nothing serious. The Confederate force at this point was much weakened by cavalry and infantry sent out to check Warren, but enough remained to be quite secure against Miles, as it turned out. The pickets left had a hard time, for, having been sent out originally for four days, provided with rations for that period only, and being necessarily left there without relief when their commands saddled up and marched after Warren, they were obliged to take up many holes in their sword-belts, as did Dugald Dalgetty, to serve instead of food. Much of the weather was cold and snowy, which added to their discomfort. The reserve pickets were kept moving about briskly, too, for their number being small they were compelled to make up for this in activity and to rush rapidly from place to place, as their services were required. There were many games of hide and seek played with the enemy—run out of a minor position, it would be retaken after a time, and then the same process repeated. Several videttes were killed at night, and there were some little incidents hardly worth relating, which, however, made an impression at the time.

On regaining a position from which a Federal picket had been driven, it was noticed that near a camp-fire the surface of the ground for about two feet square looked as if it might have been disturbed, and the idea was suggested that the enemy on retiring had concealed in the hole some large pieces of bacon or other rations rather too bulky to carry off conveniently, as they expected soon to return. This was not an uncommon practice with them. The hungry men who noticed the covered hole were very much pleased at the rich find which they thought they had discovered. One of them at once began to scrape out the earth with his hands in the lack of any implement available for the purpose, the others eagerly watching the process. Soon a clear white piece of bacon was partially uncovered, and the man paused a moment in his task with a look of great satisfaction. The others told him to "Go ahead!" which he did, but the next two or three handfuls of earth scraped out served to reveal the forehead of a corpse, and also the open, staring eyes, the waxy nose and colorless lips. There were few situations of any kind which could ruffle the equanimity of a seasoned Confederate soldier, but this was one of them. The accustomed joke, rarely lacking in any circumstances, however serious, was wanting: without a word the grave was closed, all feeling like ghouls. But no one who saw it will ever forget the complex expression on the face of the man who did the digging, though none had the stomach to laugh.

There was an occurrence on picket one night that was amusing. The Confederate videttes were all driven in, and obliged to ride hard to save themselves. One of the number was noted for owning a very nice horse, a particularly easy-keeper, remaining in condition wonderfully well on a spare supply of forage. Many advantageous "swaps" with good "boot" had frequently been offered for this animal, but none would be listened to. On this occasion, however, hardly had the owner succeeded in galloping up to the reserve picket-post, horse and man panting and blowing, before he offered to "swap" with any one on easy terms.

"He's a good 'un," said he, "but I don't

want no slow hoss for this business." The by-standers all must have agreed with him, for they declined the offer

Another incident occurred which showed generosity on one side and courage on the other. One morning the Confederates had a little force, dismounted, holding some pretty strong works on the farther side of an open field. The enemy reconnoitred with a squadron or two mounted on gray horses, coming up to within perhaps three hundred yards of these works. Fire was not opened on them because it was expected they would dismount and attack. Meantime one of the officers, riding a large gray horse, cantered leisurely across the field to within one hundred yards of the position, and there stopped for some little time calmly surveying the fortifications. Most of the men there must have been visible to him. Not a gun was fired at him all this time, though it was such an easy shot that a child could have killed him. He ought to have been shot, of course, for he was gaining knowledge of the works, but every man there admired his pluck and shrank from being the one to do the deed, leaving the unpleasant duty to someone else. Not a rifle was fired until he had turned and cantered back some distance, when there were two half-hearted, futile shots, and only two. It was probably as clear a case of generous respect for courage as was ever witnessed.

At this time, besides the Warren raid with over 34,000 troops of all arms, and the attempt of Brigadier-General (then brevet major-general of volunteers) Nelson A. Miles at Hatcher's run, Ben. Butler, on the north side of the James, was ordered to assume a threatening attitude to prevent Lee from detaching men, and this was to be carried farther, if circumstances favored. This he did not make his customary fuss in doing, being busy with a grand pyrotecnic exhibition he was preparing, such as was never tried before (nor since), which was to level the walls of the forts protecting Wilmington, like those of Jericho of old. This was in connection with a large force sent to capture Wilmington. Then it was also contemplated, if Lee's lines seemed much weakened by men drawn off to meet these four movements, to try to break through the fortifications by a *coup de main*, and capture Petersburg. All this is now revealed to us by the despatches accessible. Thus, there were five separate attempts against Lee on foot at the same time, and to each could be assigned an army almost as large as his. It is no doubt convenient for a commander to be able to muster separate armies at will, but what shall we say of the genius of his opponent, who holds them all at bay?

Warren started on his expedition early in the morning of December 7th, striking for Stony creek, on the Weldon road, intending to proceed southward, destroying the track. On the next day 851 stragglers from his columns were brought into the Federal lines, to the great disgust of the authorities, who were put to it to devise adequate punishment and means of prevention in future, and these were much discussed. To prevent "straggling" and "shirking" in line of battle on comparatively open ground the expedient of a file behind with fixed bayonets often worked well, but in thick cover ("woods-fighting") this could not be managed. The Federal generals were greatly annoyed, too, during all the previous summer and autumn by desertions. When the hostile lines came close together, sometimes separated by hardly more than a pistol-shot in distance, it was easy for men to run across, particularly at night, and this they often did, not only singly, but a dozen or more together. This practice became so frequent that a general order was issued promising every man a twenty-days' furlough who would shoot a comrade in the act of deserting.

Gaining information of Warren's movement on December 7th, Hampton started his two divisions in pursuit. Butler had some pretty fair skirmishing that morning. The intention was to prevent the enemy reaching Bellefield (Hicksford). At one o'clock P M., Hampton received a telegram from General Lee informing him that Hill, with his corps, was marching through Dinwiddie Courthouse towards Bellefield, and instructing him to communicate with Hill. This he did, explaining the position of Warren's forces, and pointing out the way in which he thought he could be intercepted. Skirmishing continued during the day, interfering with the destruction of the railroad. At two o'clock A. M. December 9th the cavalry were put in motion and arrived near Hicksford by daylight, when preparations were at once made to defend the place and protect the bridge over the Meherrin river. Colonel Garnett was in command there with a few hundred infantrymen. The enemy did not make his appearance until about three P M. the next day, when he attacked. The horse-artillery batteries of Hart and McGregor opened a sharp fire in connection with Garnett's men and repulsed the Federals, who made no further assault, though firing continued until dark. After consultation with General Hill, it was determined that Hampton would, in the morning, get round the enemy's left flank, and thus to their rear, while Hill would strike him from Jarratt station, some ten miles farther to the north. But the Federals prevented these manœuvres by retreating. They were followed up and much harassed, about 300 prisoners and many arms were taken by the cavalry, and the opportunities of the enemy to injure the railroad track curtailed, but they finally regained their lines. Meantime much anxiety was felt about Warren at Federal headquarters, and reinforcements were sent out to render him assistance. A despatch from Meade to General Grant, exhibiting some nervousness, adds: "If Warren's men will fight, and we have any luck, Warren ought to repulse him." This would not be an unnatural expectation, inasmuch as if Hill's entire corps had been there by the return of November 30th, about 15,000 strong, and Hampton's corps at the same date, including Dearing's brigade temporarily attached, about 6,000 in number, less dismounted men of over 1,000, there would have been about 20,000 in all against Warren, who had over 34,000. But in point of fact, there were not more than 16,000 Confederates in all available, as the right flank could not spare nearly all the cavalry and so large a number of infantry. Hill's troops were very badly supplied with shoes, and as the weather was cold and there was much snow and ice, they suffered great hardships. In some places the snow bore the marks of their bleeding feet.

The injury inflicted upon the Weldon railroad by Warren was small in proportion to the preparations made for the expedition and the force employed. What was effected cost the Federals much trouble and expense, and the Confederates set about repairing it at once, and without difficulty. The rails had not been destroyed. The cavalry, except Dearing's brigade, were moved down to camps near Bellefield for the purpose of restoring the railroad where broken, and also to enable them more easily to procure forage for the horses, and near that place headquarters were established. There were, during the rest of the month, no movements of the Federals of a serious character to cause hard work for the cavalry, and their labors were consequently confined chiefly to picketing, which was not very onerous. The condition of the horses improved very much during this comparative rest, and the number of the men increased as those recovered from wounds reported back. By the return of October 20, 1864, the corps, with Dearing's brigade, numbered 5,375 men, including the dismounted, and by the return of December 31, 1864, it had increased to 7,063. The efficiency of the command was much greater at the end of the campaign than it had been at the beginning, or probably at any intermediate period. Its *morale* and physique were excellent. Besides this, there were about a thousand men absent on horse-furloughs, and when these returned, together with the fresh recruits which would have been brought to camp by them, the strength of the corps for the next campaign would have been very satisfactory. But this was not to be, for events quite outside of the lines of the Army of Northern Virginia were moulding their destiny

Early in January it was decided to send Butler's and Young's brigades, of Major-General M. C. Butler's division, to Columbia, S. C., these brigades numbering by the return of December 20, 1864, 940 and 586 men respectively. This was done in order to supply troops to check Sherman as well as to give the men an opportunity to procure fresh mounts at home with the expectation of returning to Virginia in the spring. On January 19th an order was issued to this effect "The men will take with them their arms, their cooking utensils and equipments, and will be prepared for a winter campaign." Thus was terminated the campaign, and thus ended forever the service of Butler's division with the Army of Northern Virginia, of which they were proven a worthy part.

General Hampton, too, was directed to proceed to South Carolina to superintend the mounting and recruiting of the cavalry there, "with permission, if a suitable command be given him, to operate it until recalled to Virginia." At about this time he was commissioned a lieutenant-general.

Thus had closed the campaign of '64, during which Lee's numbers and material resources were almost incredibly less than those of his adversary, and yet the campaign was a victory for Lee. And if it could have been left to the Army of Northern Virginia and the Armies of the Potomac and of the James to fight out the issue as in a duel between themselves, the Southern Confederacy, as it now, in the light of information but recently accessible, seems clear, would have established its independence. That such was not the result was due to causes outside of the Virginian armies, chiefly to the unnecessary wrecking of the western Confederate army, and consequently the easy march permitted to Sherman for devastating the country and forming a junction with Grant. This was rendered possible by mismanagement, and was not the inevitable consequence of larger numbers. The theory most current at present, and which it is considered in some quarters patriotic to hold, is that the largest armies insure success in war to the side possessing them, and the result of our Civil War is pointed to as an incontrovertible illustration of this, but as a matter of fact the campaign of '64 and the war itself are proofs of the reverse of such a proposition. And it will be a sad day for these United States if their population should ever become imbued with the belief that numbers alone insure success in war, for this would signify that they were no longer able to maintain their freedom against all comers, and therefore unworthy to retain it. God forbid that they should believe all they are told in these times about the overwhelming effect of mechanical appliances in war, nitro-powders and breech-loaders, long-range artillery and high-power explosive projectiles, iron-clads and steam, annihilating distance, and that the element of the individual man is of little importance. Just so the ancients deplored that human valor was no longer of avail against the catapult, and later on, with the advent of gunpowder, "villainous saltpetre," the elimination of the human principle in battle was declared complete. Yet in spite of all this, the Macedonian phalanx and the crack Roman legions continued to hold their ground "like a stone wall," and the English archers at Agincourt and many another field, with long-bow and cloth-yard shaft played havoc with Frenchmen; and their lineal descendants, handling the antiquated muzzle-loader with Minie bullets, proved, from the Wilderness to Five Forks, that they were "chips of the old block." Mechanical inventions cause changes in details and modifications of methods in war, but the grand underlying principles remain eternal, and of these, the courage and disciplined intelligence, the moral and physical endurance of "the man behind the gun," are the most important.

The question of the *morale* of Butler's division, that part of the cavalry of the Army of Northern Virginia which at the break-up at the end of the war was attached to Johnston's army, does not, strictly speaking, belong to this narrative of the campaign of '64. Yet, as it does concern a well-earned reputation for soldierly qualities, reference to it here can hardly be deemed out of place.

Joseph Wheeler, a major-general at the time alluded to, was serving under Lieutenant-General Hampton, but his command was confined to the cavalry which accompanied him from the West after the wrecking of the army there by the gallant but ill-starred Hood. About the sentiments and condition of his own men Wheeler would naturally be supposed to be well informed, and his opinion that they were far from enthusiastically in favor of continuing the war may be correct as to many of them, but with Butler's division he did not come directly in contact, and possessed no sources of information about it, and he certainly has fallen into a great error when he states in an article in the May number of this year (1898) of the *Century Magazine* that these men were not in good heart, and could not have been depended upon at that juncture to volunteer as an escort for Jefferson Davis. Certainly nothing could be farther from the actual facts. They could have been relied upon for any enterprise that Hampton wished them to engage in, and would have felt especially honored at having the protection of Mr. Davis' person entrusted to them, and would have defended him against all odds. This is not the place to attempt a description of the career of this division in the campaign of the Carolinas in 1865, but by way of showing what condition they were in at a time not far from that of which General Wheeler speaks, it

A favorite tree of General Hampton, in the grounds at Millwood.

(395)

would be but fair to relate one of their last acts, the capture of Kilpatrick's camp near Fayetteville, N. C., on March 10, 1865.

The 9th of March had been a rainy day and the night was very dark. Somewhat in advance of the head of his division was riding General Butler, and accompanying him in column of fours were a few men constituting his escort, and a scout or two. As the horses' feet went slushing through the mire, the sound of other hoofs, muffled by mud, coming from the opposite direction was heard, and silently the command was halted by whispers passed back down the line. When the new-comers had reached within a few yards of Butler, his clear, calm voice broke through the darkness enveloping everything:

"Halt! Who comes there?"

To this was made, in the usual way, the reply that it was a detachment from a certain Ohio regiment ordered to picket that road, the speaker supposing he was talking to friends. So Butler quietly told him to march on, which the detachment proceeded to do by separating in column of twos, and thus passing on either side of the body which they had met. But when they had marched sufficiently far to be inextricably trapped, came the words from Butler, spoken in a cool, ordinary tone of voice

"Halt there! You are prisoners!"

And without another word each Confederate laid one hand on the fellow next him, with pistol ready in the other, and the whole thing was done without any fuss or noise. There were forty of them. One of their captors was a boy far from out of his teens, who rode a little plantation "tackey" not over thirteen hands in height. He was obliged to stand in his stirrups and stretch up to do it, but succeeded in collaring a big, strapping Westerner over six feet tall, with the words, uttered in a tone appropriate to some tragedy being acted on the stage,

"You are my prisoner! Surrender, sir!"

He had only left the maternal nest and joined the command a short time before this, and had no arms except a pistol which some one had loaned him, and the minute animal he bestrode so proudly could hardly be called a horse, but he was allowed from his capture to mount and arm himself satisfactorily, and was highly delighted.

Butler promptly communicated with Hampton, and they conferred together. Scouts dismounted, felt their way down the road in the direction from which the pickets had come, and discovered that the information obtained from some of the prisoners was correct, and that Kilpatrick's division was in camp near by, with nothing at all between it and Butler's division, the detachment captured having been counted upon for picketing that road. During all the night, along the edges of the road in the darkness close up to the Federal camp, lurked the trusty scouts of Hampton, so as to pick up noiselessly any one coming from there to visit the picket-post, and two or three were thus gathered in before morning, but without the firing of a shot or other sound. In some woods on each side of the road the division bivouacked, horses remaining saddled, men awake to keep them quiet, or dozing, sitting on the ground with bridle-rein in hand, or under leg, ready to mount at a second's notice. No fire must be lit for warmth or cooking and no match struck for a pipe ; so ran the orders, for this is to be a surprise-party pure and simple.

Early that morning one man had been despatched with a message, but before he reached the command for which it was intended it had moved off, and he had been trying all day to find it without success until towards evening. He had narrowly missed several times riding into detachments of the enemy, and been shot at more than once for his trouble, and at about ten o'clock at night rejoined his comrades, hungry, tired, wet, and disgusted. The first thing he did was to "borrow" a piece of corn bread which had been fresh when the world was younger, and a canteen of water which was rich in all manner of germs, but uncontaminated by whiskey. He then looked about, as well as the darkness would permit, and found several of his friends in a group together earnestly whispering, their horses standing round looking as solemn and wise as judges on the bench. Now, these young men ought undoubtedly to have been engaged in saying their prayers and softly humming snatches of hymns recalled from early days, for the purpose of bracing up their nerves for the fight fixed for daylight, but the truth must be told, and the words overheard by the hungry, tired trooper just arrived were:

"It is she! I know it is!"

"By Jove! Certain?"

"Yes! I tracked the wheels for hours to-day. No chance to mistake the wheel-marks of that victoria among these heavy wagon-trains. She is in his camp, and we will be sure to see her in the morning."

Then they all whispered "By Jove!" with great earnestness.

It seems there was an exceedingly pretty young girl in Columbia when these boys had been there lately, whom some of them had been acquainted with. She dressed very well and drove in a victoria at a time when it was not *comme il faut* to dress well and drive in victorias. With her mother she had left Columbia, as a refugee, with Sherman's army. To anticipate: after her arrival at the North, hers was a far from quiet career. At Newport, the Mecca of the faithful to fashion, she figured; married into a rich family of Puritan extraction; released "*a vinculo*," remarried, after sundry experiences, within foreign diplomatic circles, and "raised Cain" generally. That, however, does not concern this story, but her connection with it will appear from the sequel on the morrow.

This opportunity to strike Kilpatrick was just what was desired, for his command blocked the roads to Fayetteville on the Cape Fear river, about eight miles distant, where a crossing was intended, and a successful attack would remove him out of the way Hampton's plan was by the first daylight to burst into camp by the unpicketed road, surprising and throwing into confusion the Federal cavalry division, and Wheeler was instructed, when he heard the firing, to drive in the pickets opposite to him and break through to assist Butler. By this it was expected to hem in a large number of prisoners, and hold the position until everything removable could be brought off and the rest burned.

Before daylight Butler's command was noiselessly formed in the road in column of fours, the portion to which was assigned the leading charge being advanced considerably beyond the others, and consequently close to the camp to be attacked, leaving a good interval between them and the troops behind, which admitted of the latter being promptly dismounted in case of a counter-attack. The ground was soaked and steaming with exhalations, and the fog rendered it difficult to see, even after sunrise. When the proper moment arrived, the detachment intended to lead the charge was moved on a walk almost to the entrance of the camp, and there halted for a moment as Butler rode to their head. Removing his hat and waving it above his head, he spoke, in ringing tones:

"Troops from Virginia! Follow me! Forward, march!" and then "Charge!"

They thundered into the sleeping camp, and if all the foul fiends from the nether world had accompanied them the Federals could not have been more surprised or demoralized. The camp-guards, if there were any awake, had no time to give warning, and the men under the tent-flies were literally ridden over; or, as they sprang out half-asleep, were sabred or ridden down before they knew what was doing. Undressed and unarmed, awakened out of a profound sleep to find their camp overrun, they fled in all directions, leaving accoutrements behind. It was a wild sight. When the Confederates had charged through the ground they wheeled and came rushing back, scattering and riding down what was left, and making prisoners. Meantime other detachments of the division had struck the position at different points, and were making themselves heard from most effectually.

Just then a pathetic incident occurred. Some prisoners, mostly broken-down stragglers from the infantry, or citizen-soldiery, in charge of the Federal provost guard, 173 in number, seeing that rescue was at hand, broke from their captors and rushed forward to meet their friends, adding to the tumult by their cheers and cries of joy. Two of these, in their excitement, recognizing mounted comrades advancing, threw their arms around the necks of their horses and were thus killed, being in the obscurity and smoke mistaken for enemies. One was so slain by a loving friend. It was the most painful occurrence ever witnessed by those present.

From these escaped prisoners it was quickly learned that a small farm-house on the right of the road, where it entered the camp, was headquarters. This house had been passed and left behind by the regiments opening the attack, for, as stated, it was difficult to make out objects clearly in the uncertain light. Thus had been afforded an opportunity for Kilpatrick and his staff to escape. This general himself fled in his shirt and drawers, and so failed to be recognized and captured. Close to this house were fastened many horses, among others those belonging to headquarters, all of which were carried off, except such as were accidentally shot. A handsome black, and a peculiar-looking piebald stallion belonging to Kilpatrick, were taken, as was also a third. One of the pluckiest of pistol-duels came off just here. A Federal from about headquarters cut loose a fine horse, and leaping on his back was about making off, but finding an enemy close in upon him, turned about, and the two fought it out, no one interfering, but, on the contrary, several stopped in their own work to look on, for the episode occupied only a few seconds. Although so close together that they could almost touch, each fired several shots before the Federal rolled off his horse, as he fell on the animal's neck delivering bravely one last shot in dying.

Some of the Federals, thus summarily expelled from their camp, communicated the news of their misfortune to their infantry, which was set in motion for their succor. The plan had been, as we have said, that when the noise of Butler's attack was heard by General Joseph Wheeler, he should drive in the pickets and strike the camp from another direction, and thus co-operate with Butler. This he failed to do in the manner expected, being delayed by some swampy ground, as it was then alleged, and by the time he came up the Federals had had a breathing spell for rallying and an opportunity to send for assistance. Kilpatrick, too, was exerting in creditable manner his utmost personal endeavors to save his command from the utter ruin which seemed imminent. Thus a pretty stiff fight of dismounted men was soon under way, and artillery opened on both sides.

About this time, at the entrance-door of the headquarter house, a female skirt, a hat and ribbon and other similar accoutrements of the fair sex appeared, and were at once spied by some of those young fellows who had been found whispering together the night before. The first duty of the cavalier is to rescue distressed damsels, and so these boys thoroughly believed, and were about delightedly so to do. But, alas! for all human hopes. On nearer inspection this proved to be the wrong damsel, if damsel she could be termed at all, being old, ugly, and perhaps respectable, and she turned out to be a "school-marm" from Vermont, who had availed herself of the assistance of Sherman's army to return to her home. However, she was a woman after all, if she was ugly, and one of those same thoughtless youngsters referred to, quietly dismounted, and, hat in hand, approached her, bowing as deferentially as if it indeed had been the hoped-for fair one, and kindly explained the danger from chance bullets and shells against which the thin weather-boarding of the house would be little better protection than pasteboard. But, woman-like, she could not at first be made to comprehend that the horses could not be attached to her vehicle and she drive quietly away to more congenial scenes. However, at length she took in the situation sensibly, and was conducted to a drainage-ditch, in which she lay and was comparatively safe. Fortunately she was not hurt during the *melee*, and seemed somewhat appreciative of the kindness done her. But it was all a sad disappointment to those expectant boys.

During all the hurly-burly of the fight Butler was calmly directing the operations of his command. Like "Chinese" Gordon, who carried no weapons in action, only a bamboo cane in his hand, Butler during this campaign was always to be seen among the bullets, with merely a lady's silver-mounted riding-whip, with which he would point out from time to time to those around him what was to be done.

A large number of horses were safely carried off, and a considerable amount of arms, accoutrements, and clothing, and some wagons, but not as many of the latter as would otherwise have been secured, because of the stampeding of the animals pertaining to them. The same cause operated against hauling away artillery. This could have been effected if Wheeler had succeeded in carrying out the part of the programme assigned to him. But, as it turned out, time, as we have said, was allowed the enemy for rallying and procuring help from their infantry before Butler was reinforced. General Joseph E. Johnston, in referring to this affair in his "Narrative," says that more wagons and artillery were not brought off because the men stopped to plunder; but this was not correct—at least, of Butler's division. It was true as to a part of Wheeler's command, which was not under the best of discipline. Besides the Confederate prisoners released, numbering 173, there were over 500 Federals captured and taken away. The killed and wounded of the enemy must have exceeded 300, and these, added to the number of captured Federals and released Confederates, would make the aggregate of nearly 1,000, which was more than the entire force of Butler. Kilpatrick's division was about 5,000 strong. Wheeler's command numbered some 3,000, if the men could be got together. The work done, Hampton withdrew to occupy the roads leading to Fayetteville, which he had thus cleared of obstruction. The losses were small, but unfortunately General Butler's brother, serving on his staff, lost his arm.

This affair attracted much attention at the time, and had quite a bad effect upon the *morale* of Kilpatrick's cavalry division. That officer, in talking the matter over after the war with one who had been present at the fight, said that as he was making his escape, with his command scattering in every direction, he thought, "Well! I have been working hard these four years for a major-general's commission and now in five minutes I have lost it all." He was at this time only brevet major-general. This disaster probably weakened him in his commanding general's estimation, for soon after this Sherman paid his visit to Grant at Petersburg, and was very urgent in his request to have Sheridan assigned to him. In fact, he persuaded Grant to consent to this, but at Sheridan's earnest remonstrance this arrangement was postponed, though not altogether abandoned. The surprise and rout of his camp by Hampton, "the first terrible onset of the foe," as Kilpatrick terms it, was particularly mortifying to him because of the similar misfortune he had suffered at the hands of the same unwelcome visitor hardly more than a year before at Atlee's station during the Dahlgren raid, when he was obliged to seek refuge in the bosom of Ben. Butler, and thence embark aboard ship to regain the lines of his army.

He naturally felt very sore upon the subject. It is not, therefore, to be wondered at that in his official report he should not have quite conformed to the accounts given by eye-witnesses of the affair, and those conversant with the facts. He says that Hampton charged his camp with three divisions, but, as has been related, the attack was made by Butler's division only, so that, instead of being outnumbered, Kilpatrick actually had five to one. Of course the surprise effected placed the Federals under a great disadvantage. In his official report he says: "Hampton led the centre division (Butler's), and in less than a minute had driven back my people and taken possession of my headquarters, captured the artillery, and the whole command was flying before the most formidable cavalry charge I ever have witnessed. Colonel Spencer and a large portion of my staff were virtually taken prisoners. On foot I succeeded in gaining the cavalry camp a few hundred yards in the rear and found the men fighting with the rebels for their camp and animals, and we were finally forced back some 500 yards farther to a swamp impassable to friend or foe." This, except in regard to Butler's division being the centre instead of the entire attacking force, is substantially correct. What, however, he goes on to say about recapturing the camp is somewhat erroneous. Hampton naturally withdrew when he concluded he had effected all that was practicable, not intending to engage in a battle with all the infantry as well as cavalry of Sherman's army. Kilpatrick estimates that he lost eighty-seven officers and men, besides an additional number not specified, who were less seriously wounded, and 103 prisoners, but the latter number does not correspond with the prisoners carried away by the Confederates, who counted up over 500, and in casualties a similar mistake has probably been made.

Besides, there were other similar matters to which General Kilpatrick did not relish reference, practical jokes at his expense by Hampton, especially the "Buckland races" in Fauquier county, Virginia, which came off on October 19, 1863. Hampton, with his division, was then at Buckland, confronting Kilpatrick's cavalry and a considerable force of infantry. The enemy was endeavoring to cross southward the Broad run at Buckland. Fitz. Lee's division was some miles off but within supporting distance, and the following plan was accordingly arranged. Hampton withdrew in the direction of Warrenton for nearly five miles, and Kilpatrick, supposing him to be retreating, crossed Broad run and followed. Fitz. Lee's division was then moved up so as to be interposed between the Federals and the ford in their rear It was a case of the spider and the fly. Kilpatrick, however, had been cautious about putting his whole foot in the trap, and left

Ruins of Millwood, General Hampton's home near Columbia, S. C. Destroyed by Sherman's armies.

Custer's brigade behind at Buckland at the ford. So Fitz. Lee coming up fell upon Custer, and a stiff fight ensued. At the sound of the firing, Hampton at once wheeled about, as had been agreed upon, and dashed furiously at Kilpatrick, whose men, realizing from the sounds of musketry and artillery in their rear proceeding from the combat between Fitz. Lee and Custer, that the trap had been sprung, made but slight resistance and endeavored to effect a retreat, but soon broke in wild disorder This quickly became a stampede on the part of Davies' brigade. Colonel Young, commanding Butler's brigade, endeavored to cut off the enemy by galloping his troops through the woods on the right of the road, and Rosser charged on the left, while Gorden's brigade made all speed down the road in direct pursuit. And thus they raced for nearly five miles. Some of the fugitives from Davies' brigade crossed the run, and the rest made towards

Haymarket. Eight wagons and ambulances were captured, among them Custer's headquarter wagon, baggage and papers, and 250 prisoners from Davies' brigade. Custer, perceiving a dense cloud of dust and a clatter of hoofs approaching from the direction of Warrenton, had concluded he had better recross the run before the stampede reached him, and this he succeeded in doing without allowing his command to fall into much disorder, and safely carrying away his artillery. But the rest of Kilpatrick's cavalry required much looking-up before they were found, as they did not stop their swift gallop through the exhilarating October air until reaching the lines of their First army corps. In the Federal official reports of this affair no mention is made of the stampede of Davies' brigade, but the fact remains established by numerous witnesses on both sides in the fight.

Apropos of all this is the following anecdote:

On April 13, 1865, General Joseph E. Johnston had an interview at Greensboro, N. C., with Mr. Davis and his Cabinet, and as a consequence General Johnston was directed to send a communication, then prepared and signed by him, to General Sherman, requesting a conference. General Johnston late that night sent this note to General Hampton, then near Hillsboro, with the request that it be delivered by a member of his staff. General Hampton was not informed of the contents of the communication. He awoke Captain Rawlins Lowndes, of his staff, and entrusted the document to him to be delivered. As it was then after midnight and very dark and rainy, the General suggested that it was not unlikely Lowndes might be fired upon by the Federal cavalry pickets before he could communicate to them the nature of his mission, and said he could take as escort a company, or a squadron, if he wished it. Lowndes replied that an escort would be of no benefit to him, and that he did not think it advisable to expose the men to the risk of fire without good cause. So the General then told him to take with him one reliable man as courier, and to bring back a reply to the note he would deliver. Lowndes consequently started accompanied by a courier, and soon reached Kilpatrick's lines without misadventure, and was duly halted by a vidette. He stated his business, the officer in charge of the post was summoned, and a message sent to Kilpatrick's headquarters, to which, in reply, Lowndes was invited to repair. The letter to Sherman was forwarded, but as that officer was at a distance, eight hours elapsed before his answer was delivered to be carried back to Hampton. In the meantime Lowndes remained a guest at Kilpatrick's headquarters. They talked about various things, quite amicably, of course, but after awhile the conversation fell upon military matters, and some of them were disposed to chaff Lowndes rather much. Kilpatrick was still very sore indeed concerning that early morning visit Hampton had paid him unannounced only about a month before, and showed it rather too much, implying that a meeting of that kind with notice would have resulted differently. This nettled Lowndes, so he said:

"Well, General, I make you the following proposition, and I will pledge myself that General Hampton will carry it out in every respect. You, with your staff, take 1,500 men, and General Hampton, with his staff, will meet you with 1,000 men, all to be armed with the sabre alone. The two parties will be drawn up mounted in regimental formation opposite to each other, and, at a signal to be agreed upon, will charge. That will settle the question which are the best men."

They all laughed, but did not accept the proposal, and said they would consider it. Perhaps such an arrangement was impracticable, but, all the same, it is a pity the affair could not have come off. It would have made a pleasant ending to the war. At that time none of them knew that their sabres were practically sheathed forever. If they had known this at the time, possibly the meeting might have been managed in spite of difficulties. The last word Lowndes said at leave-taking was to repeat his proposition to his hosts.

When it became known by the cavalry that a surrender of Johnston's army would probably be decided upon, there was great repugnance to acquiescing in it, and many officers and men were not included in the capitulation. Notable among these was General Hampton. A considerable number of minor officers and privates desired to pass over into the trans-Mississippi department, there to continue the war under his leadership, and started thither for that purpose. It was not until he had let it be known that he had abandoned the intention of further resistance that the proposed muster in the West was given up. At the time the project of furnishing an escort to Mr. Davis, to enable him to make his escape, was under consideration, Hart's battery of horse artillery volunteered almost to a man for the purpose; indeed, the very guns, eloquent during all these four years in every fight within their reach in Virginia and the Carolinas, seemed to long to join their voices in thunderous assent to the proposition, "Will you volunteer?" So much for the *morale* of Butler's division.

Thus was ended the career of Hampton as soldier, but not so the method of cavalry fighting which he may be justly said to have introduced, and which others learned from him and utilized. But though his achievements in war, which had won for him fame with foe as well as friend, were terminated, his wise and patriotic work as pacificator was destined to gain for him the deep gratitude of his own people, as well it might, and the approbation of all Americans.

Our country has now emerged, for better or for worse, from a life of peaceful occupations: she is no longer content to be farmer, manufacturer, and merchant—the honest, useful industries to which she had, as far as practicable, hitherto confined herself during all the years of her political existence. Now she has essayed to embark in foreign wars and conquests, and must assume the responsibility which the changed conditions render necessary. Our recent demonstration against Spain has not in fact been, properly speaking, a war at all. "Dramatic" it may have been, a term which General Shafter, in all seriousness, applied to it in an official communication to the War Department, but perhaps melodramatic would have been an even more appropriate word. War it was not, for the essential of fighting was lacking, there being no foe worthy of the name with whom to fight. Hamlet was conspicuously absent from the programme, and of strategy there was still less. "Privations" there may have been, in the sense of the missing of accustomed comforts by home-bred boys (good timber for army-making when seasoned), but the most meagre rations ever issued at the "front" in Cuba would have been considered a feast of Lucullus by the Confederate soldier. Yet, although this affair has been "a walk-over," its consequences will be out of all proportion in importance, and unless the teachings of history are fallacious, it will prove the forerunner of real and tragic struggles. With Asia, as well as Europe, our country must prepare herself, when necessary, to grapple. In time, not merely "little wars" with "anæmic" nations, but serious contests must be expected, in which numbers and resources will not be, as heretofore, overwhelmingly in her favor. Then she must find compensation for lack of numerical strength, not in the delusive fad of the day, "sea-power," "proud navies laughing at the storm," but in the brain and manhood of her sons. From Philip's armada and Bonaparte's armies England was preserved not by huge English ships, but by hard-fighting English men. If it ever happens in the future, as well it may, that the countless millions of Asia, taught European strategy and tactics, equipped with modern iron-clads on sea and magazine rifles on land, allied perhaps with ambitious western nations, and under the leadership of some second Napoleon, shall swarm upon our shores for the purpose of blotting out our religion and representative government, will not our descendants then, standing together in their hour of need, irrespective of the side on which their ancestors fought in our Civil War, pray to the god of battles to raise up a Robert E. Lee to command their armies, and a Hampton to handle the cavalry? But Providence usually helps those only who help themselves. Is it not advisable, then, to study the methods of the leaders, and to learn of the courage and endurance of the soldiers which made the campaign of "1864" in splendor inferior to none recorded in history?

"Lord God of Hosts, be with us yet,
Lest we forget! lest we forget!"

THE END.

INDEX.

	PAGE.
Alger, Colonel Fifth Michigan cavalry,	165
Armament of the cavalry of the Army of Northern Virginia,	91, 96
Armament of the cavalry of the Army of the Potomac,	94
Army of Northern Virginia,	78, 104, 130, 136
Army of the Potomac,	78, 108, 109, 126, 134, 176 to 185
Army of the James, commanded by Ben. Butler,	231
Army of Johnston's—at Fayetteville, 30; conference with Sherman, 421; surrender,	424
Army and Navy Gazette, extract from issue of October 8, 1864,	321
Ashland, fight at,	173
Bancroft, George, historian,	18
Bamberg, Lieutenant,	52
"Baby-eater,"	61
Barker, Major Theodore G., A. A. G.,	265, 335
Bear hunter, Hampton as,	47

INDEX.

Belfield, cavalry headquarters at, 387
Blackwater river, 289, 303
Brandy Station, battle of, 68
Breech-loaders, 92, 147
"Buckland Races," 416
Butler's brigade, 126, 142, 157, 158, 162, 166, 167, 168, 170, 171, 172, 213, 278, 388
Butler's division, 277, 318, 338, 339, 388, 389, 393 to 425
Butler, General Ben. F., 114, 115, 244, 314, 317, 327, 356, 368, 381
Butler, General Matthew Calbraith, 33, 52, 63, 67, 68, 71, 142, 170, 203, 279, 333, 334, 373, 397, 404, 410
Burgess Mill, battle of, 323, 335 to 344

Cashier's Valley (Hampton mountain home), 38 to 41, 44, 45
Cattle-raid, 288
Cavalry of the Army of Northern Virginia, 78 to 104, 137, 142 to 146, 147 to 152, 267, 268 to 270, 358
Cavalry of the Army of the Potomac, 94, 134, 146, 147, 267, 268, 359
Challenge to Kilpatrick, 423
Chambliss, General, killed, 272, 274

INDEX.

Chambliss' brigade,	145, 217, 245
Chew, Major,	204, 237, 341
Chambersburg raid,	56 to 68
City Point, headquarters Army of the Potomac,	287, 288
Cobb Legion,	52, 142
Comparison between Hampton and Sheridan,	223 to 228
Conner, General James,	52, 284
Cold Harbor, battle of,	175 to 181
Conscription,	314
Cotton crop of Hampton in 1860,	46
Custer, General,	162, 198, 199, 213, 419, 420
Dahlgren raid,	108 to 123
Davis, Jefferson, escort of, 394; conference with General Johnston,	421
Day, David, the spy,	35
Dearing's brigade,	269, 330, 336
Diary of a Federal prisoner taken at Trevilian,	212, 213
Dunovant, General, 278; death,	321
Duties of the cavalry,	81
Eutaw, battle of,	10
Eleventh Virginia cavalry,	142

INDEX.

Fair lady, 402
Fayetteville, charge of Hampton at, 30 to 36
Five Forks, battle of, 324, 358 to 361; organization and strength of cavalry corps at, 358; strength of the Federal force at, 359; letter of Lee to Hampton about, dated August 1, 1865, 361, 362
Fisherman, Hampton as, 41 to 43
Fontaine, Doctor, death of, 322
Forage of the cavalry, 99 to 102
Forrest, Lieutenant-General, 151
Fourth South Carolina cavalry, 142
First North Carolina cavalry, 52, 145
First Virginia cavalry, 142
Fourth Virginia cavalry, 142
Fifth Virginia cavalry, 145
Fifteenth Virginia cavalry, 145
Fifth North Carolina cavalry, 145
Fifth South Carolina cavalry, 142

Gary, General, 52, 217
Gary's brigade, 146, 171, 217, 219, 220, 270, 273
Gettysburg, 72 to 75
Gorden, General, 138
Gorden's brigade, 138, 145, 419
Gregg, General, 146, 218, 219, 220, 267, 270

Gregg, strength of division, 326, 369
Graham's battery, incident in, 318, 319
Grant, General, 134; correspondence, 314; reinforcements, 325; at Burgess Mill, 346; autumn elections, 369; correspondence with Meade about Hampton, 369, 370

Halsey, Lieutenant, 52
HAMPTON, LIEUTENANT-GENERAL WADE—birth, 9; ancestry, 10 to 24; at Millwood, 24; in reconstruction, 25, 26, 27; amiability, 27; captures a naked prisoner, 27, 28, 29; at Fayetteville charge, 29 to 36; at his mountain home, 37 to 41; sportsman, 40; fisherman, 41 to 43; cotton-planter, 45 to 47; bear hunter, 47; as to States' Rights, 47 to 51; raises the Hampton Legion, 51, 52; wounded at Manassas, 51; wounded at Seven Pines, 52; transferred to cavalry as brigadier-general, 52; raid in Pope's rear, 55, 56; on Chambersburg raid, 56 to 68; Brandy Station, 68; Gettysburg, 72, 77; wounded, 75; not a "West Pointer," 76, 77; head-

quarters at Milford during winter of 1863–1864, 107; composition and strength of his division at that time, 108; marches to attack Kilpatrick and Dahlgren, 111; attacks, routs, and pursues Kilpatrick, 112 to 115; his personal knowledge of the Dahlgren papers, 121, 122; reorganization of his division, 124 to 126; at the Wilderness and Spotsylvania, 136, 137; commander of the cavalry, 142 to 146; composition of his division, 144; composition of the corps, 142; strength of Hampton's force, 146; Hampton's tactics original and new, 148, 149, 150, 151; at Hawes' Shop, 153 to 170; at Ashland fight, 173, 174; strategy of his fighting, 185; in the Trevilian campaign, 187 to 223; at Nance's Shop fight, 219 to 223; crossing James river, 223; results of Trevilian campaign, 225 to 228; routing Wilson's raiders, 231, 244; at Sappony Church fight, 237; Meade's letter to Grant about Hampton, 234; captures made from Wilson, 243 to 246; officially made corps commander, 260; change of staff, 265; fighting on north side of James river, August 16th and 17th, 270 to 273; at battle Reams Station, 278 to 283; Lee's letters about Reams Station, 284, 285; leading the cattle-raid, 284 to 303; letter from Lee about the cattle-raid, 302; fighting in the last days of September, 313 to 318; letter of Lee, 323; at battle of Burgess Mill, 324 to 350; letter to Lee and his reply, 350, 351; letter to Lee, 352 to 354; letter from Lee, 354; letter of August 1, 1865, from Lee about the effect of Hampton's absence at battle of Five Forks, 361, 362; ordered to South Carolina, 389; conference, and Johnston's despatch to Sherman, 421

Hampton, Wade, of 1776 and 1812, 10 to 17
Hampton, Wade, of Millwood, 17 to 24; his famous ride, 21, 22
Hampton, Wade, Jr., 335, 346
Hampton, Lieutenant-Colonel Frank, 68, 71
Hampton, Lieutenant William Preston, 71, 72, 335, 344, 345, 346
Hampton's brigade, composition of, 52, 55

INDEX.

Hampton's division, composition of, 107, 108, 126, 142, 145
Hampton's corps, organization of, 142 to 146
Hampton's Legion, 51
Hampton's tactics, 148, 149, 150, 151
Hart's battery, 52, 111, 204, 341, 385
Hart, captain of H. B., wounded, 341
Hartford Convention, 23, 48
Hancock, General, 277, 286, 318, 327, 330, 334, 338, 339, 357
Hawes' Shop, battle of, 154 to 170
Heth, General, 319, 334, 336
Hicksford expedition, 375, 382 to 387
Hill, General A. P., 278, 279, 280, 330, 351, 353, 354, 355, 384, 386
Hospital supplies, 341
Horse supply, 97
"Horse-swap," 379
Hunter, General, 187, 232

Inaccuracies in official returns of numbers, 102, 103, 104, 127, 267, 268, 269

Jeffords, Lieutenant-Colonel, 335
Jeff. Davis Legion, 52, 142

Kilpatrick, General, raid and rout of, 108 to 123; rout and capture of camp near Fayetteville, N. C., 397 to 415; "Buckland Races," 416 to 420

Kautz's division, 231, 240, 244

LAUREL BRIGADE, 92, 126, 142, 199, 278, 288, 313

LEE, GENERAL ROBERT E.—anecdote about, 132, 133; views about Petersburg, 183; letter from Hampton, 213; letter to Hampton about Trevilian, 227, 228; relations with Hampton, 264, 265; official letter to Hampton, 273, 274; communications to Hampton and Vance about battle of Reams Station, 285; note to Hampton about the cattle-raid, 302; correspondence with Hampton about battle of Burgess Mill, 350 to 355; letter to Hampton about battle of Five Forks, 361, 362; his retreat from Petersburg, 363 to 367; letter to Mr. Seddon, Secretary of War, 366, 367

Lee, General Fitzhugh, division, 145, 188, 200, 201, 202, 214, 220, 223, 227, 241, 242, 419

Lee, General W. H. F., division, 145, 173, 174, 188, 235, 272, 273, 320, 333, 334, 335

Lee, General Stephen D., 52
Lewis battalion, 142
Logan, General, 52
Lomax brigade, 145
Lone damsel, 408, 409, 410
Losses of Hampton in Trevilian and Wilson raids, 247
Losses of Sheridan during his command of four months, 258, 259

Madison, Mrs. James, 23, 24
Magazine rifles, 94, 147
Mahone, General, 337
McClure, A. H. K., of Philadelphia *Times*, 56 to 59
McGregor's battery, 279, 385
Meade, General—"Household troops," 109, 127, 128, 129, 134, 294, 295; letter to Grant about Hampton, 234; cattle-raid, 294, 295, 300; at Burgess Mill, 346; despatch to Grant about Hicksford expedition, 386
Miles, General Nelson A., "looking out" at Hatcher's run, 375, 376, 381
Milford, Hampton's headquarters, 107, 125
Millwood, the Hampton home, 18, 24
Mississippi, Hampton's plantations in, 45, 46

Millen's battalion,	142
Mountain home of Hampton,	37 to 41
Muzzle-loaders,	91 to 96
Naked prisoner, anecdote about,	27 to 29
Nance's Shop, battle of,	219, 220, 223
Ninth Virginia cavalry,	145, 245
New Orleans, battle of,	20, 21
Numerical strength of Federal and Confederate cavalry,	146, 147, 267 to 270
Numerical strength at Trevilian,	189, 190
Official returns, inaccuracy of,	102 to 104
Organization of Hampton's corps,	142, 145, 146
Organization of Sheridan's corps,	146, 147
Petersburg—Commencement of siege, 216; strategical position, 230; retreat from,	363 to 367
Phillips' Legion,	142
Picketing experience,	253 to 257
Pickett, General, at Five Forks,	360
Pleasanton, General,	66, 134, 149
Plucky Federal trooper,	380, 381
Pocketing a frozen eye,	374
Powder,	96

Position of the Army of Northern Virginia and the Army of Potomac at opening of the campaign of 1864, 107, 108
Premium on gold, 314

Quartermasters, 88, 91

Raid in Pope's rear, 55
Raines, Colonel, powder works of at Augusta, Ga., 96
Reconstruction period, 25, 26, 27
Rations of cavalry, 82 to 91, 427
"Records of the Union and Confederate Armies," characteristics of the, 183 to 185
Relative strength of the Army of Northern Virginia and Army of Potomac, 79, 102, 127, 130
Reams station, Federal lodgment, 274; battle of, 278 to 283
Ride of Colonel Hampton from New Orleans, 21
Rosser, General Thomas L., 92, 94, 126, 142, 152, 154, 157, 168, 173, 174, 199, 213, 278, 288, 290, 312, 313, 358, 419

Samaria Church, fight of, 218 to 223
Sappony Church, fight at, 237, 238
Scouts, 305 to 311
"Sea-power," 428

INDEX.

Secession,	47 to 51
Second North Carolina cavalry,	145
Second Virginia cavalry,	142
Seventh Georgia cavalry,	142
Seventh Virginia cavalry,	142
Sixth Virginia cavalry,	145
Sixth South Carolina cavalry,	142
Shadbourne, scout,	302

Sherman, General Tecumseh. 18, 389, 390, 413, 421 to 424

Sheridan, General, to command cavalry corps, 135; Richmond raid, 137 to 141, 146 to 149, 152 to 169; at Trevilian, 189 to 212; ordered to Shenandoah Valley, 257; criticism of, 257 to 260; numerical strength at Five Forks, 359

Stuart, General J. E. B.,	55 to 74, 107, 138, 142
Spotsylvania Courthouse, battle of,	151
Stanton, Secretary of War,	356, 357
Stony Creek raid,	370, 373
Swinton's "Army of the Potomac,"	176 to 181

Tactics of Hampton,	148, 149, 150, 151, 425
Tenth Virginia cavalry,	52, 145
Third Virginia cavalry,	142
Third North Carolina cavalry,	145

Thirteenth Virginia cavalry, 145
Twelfth Virginia cavalry, 142
Torbert, General, 146, 189, 192, 198, 212, 267
Trevilian campaign, 187 to 228; official report of Sheridan, 210, 211, 212; summary of results, 223 to 228, 359, 360

War correspondents, punishment of by Stanton, 356, 357
Warren, General, 318; at Five Forks, 360; Hicksford expedition, 375, 382, 388
West Point, 76
Wickham's brigade, 142
Wilderness, battle of, 136
Wilson, General James H., 146, 173, 174, 231 to 245, 267
Wilson raid, 231 to 245
Wheeler, Major-General Joseph, 393, 408
White's battalion, 142
White House threatened, 216
Women tending the wounded at Trevilian, 209
Wounded in the rain, 340, 341

Yellow Tavern, fight at, 138
Young, General, wounded, 174
Young's brigade, 126, 142, 174, 389

B. F. JOHNSON PUBLISHING CO., RICHMOND, VA.

SOME LEADING SCHOOL BOOKS.
Of the South.   By the South.   For the Entire Country.

NEW
IN INCEPTION, DESIGN, AND CREATION.

STAMPED WITH THE MARK OF POPULAR APPROVAL
AS WELL AS

The Commendation of Distinguished Educators.

Lee's United States Histories. "With malice towards none" the author has traced in a charming manner the birth and progress of our country up to the present time. The result of her many years' observation in the school room, and patient research outside, is a "Primary," a "New School," and a "High School" History of the United States—three splendid books, each a *complete volume*. The name of the first history explains the purpose of that book. The New School is the ideal common school history. It is an excellent volume—full, accurate, and attractive. Many illustrations adorn its well-written pages. The High School history is specially suited to the more advanced instruction of high schools, academies, and colleges. A profusion of illustrations illume its pages, and every detail of the more important historical events is recorded. The publishers of these histories have a mass of testimonials from college presidents, senators, governors, congressmen, clergymen, professors, teachers of every grade, and private citizens from all sections, praising Mrs. Lee's work. This concerted approval is very gratifying to both author and publisher, and is, we think, an evidence that their histories are superior to those the people have been using.

A FEW FACTS.

Lee's History of the United States—Primary, New School, or High School—is a library of United States histories culled, classified, brought to the touchstone of truth, with new and authenticated matter injected, and bound into one attractive volume. Facts and figures taken largely from the Official Records of the War Department and numerous other official sources. The truth of each chapter is substantiated by reputable authorities cited. Acknowledged by competent critics to be the most teachable and satisfactory school history published for years. A most valuable book of reference.

Lee's Primary School History of the United States . . . . $ .50
Lee's New School History of the United States (formerly "Brief") 75
Lee's High School History of the United States (formerly "Advanced") 1.00

 If you are interested in a United States History by the South, and for the entire country, write for descriptive circulars explaining more fully the merits of these works. Better still, send the amount of the retail price and own the book.—"Seeing is believing."

QUESTIONS.

1. What United States history does your child use?
2. Does it concern you whether or not it tells the truth?
3. Is not a truth half told more dangerous than a direct falsehood?
4. Is it not a fact that the history your child studies sins by omission as well as by commission?
5. How long will the people stand this condition of things?

B. F. Johnson Publishing Co., Richmond, Va.

SOUTHERN LITERATURE. By Miss LOUISE MANLY, of South Carolina. Over 500 pages; more than 50 full-page illustrations. Large 12mo.; cloth. Price, $1.00.

"SOUTHERN LITERATURE," by Miss Louise Manly, of South Carolina, is a comprehensive review, with copious extracts and criticisms, of the leading Southern productions in the literary world from 1579 to 1895. It contains an appendix with a full list of Southern authors; has over 500 pages, 12mo.; is illustrated with more than 50 full-page engravings, and substantially bound in cloth; is already used extensively in the schools of the South; and has made a favorable impression in the North and in the West.

This is one of the books referred to in Mr. Minter's able address before the Texas State Teachers' Association. The need for just such a work has been long felt, in both educational and literary circles. It is lamentable, but nevertheless true, that many of the best and brightest Southern writers are scarcely known outside the circle of their intimate friends. Their productions have either gone begging for a publisher, or been published by houses that felt very little interest in the author, and far less interest in his productions. But, fortunately, an avenue is now opening up for the dissemination of Southern literature; and all that is required for the permanent establishment of this much needed avenue is the *substantial* encouragement of Southern teachers, school officials, and patriotic citizens of all trades and professions.

SOUTHERN STATES OF THE AMERICAN UNION. By Dr. J. L. M. CURRY, of Virginia. 272 pages; large 12mo. Student's edition, plain cloth, $1.00; Library edition, $1.25.

THIS book is not controversial. Its aim is to reconstruct ideas and opinions adverse to the South, in so far as they are founded on ignorance and prejudice. It embodies in one neat and compact volume the result of the studies on Constitutional History of one of the ablest and most accomplished writers of this country. The writing of this book is timely. Some of the greatest political events of the past are being adjusted into truthful history, and new light is being added by the facile pen of a man whose master mind analyzes with the clearness and power of a spectrum. This book should have a place in the curriculum of every high-school, academy, college, and university of this country. The schools of the South can ill afford to be without it. Every citizen should have a copy in his library.

WILLIAMSON'S LIFE OF GENERAL ROBERT E. LEE. By Mrs. M. L. WILLIAMSON, of New Market, Va. Nearly 200 pages, beautifully and profusely illustrated. 12mo. Illuminated covers. Price, 25 cents. Library edition, cloth, gold stamping, 75 cents.

THE only history of that grand, good man written specially for the young. The style in which the book is written secures one's interest from the start and never lets it lag. The profuse illustrations delight older people. The book was intended originally as a gift book, but is now adapted to schools as well. The low price at which we offer it places it within the reach of all.

WILLIAMSON'S LIFE OF GENERAL "STONEWALL" JACKSON. By Mrs. M. L. WILLIAMSON, of New Market, Va. Nearly 200 pages, beautifully and profusely illustrated. 12mo. Illuminated covers. Price, 25 cents. Library edition, cloth, gold stamping, 75 cents.

THE very flattering reception given Mrs. Williamson's Life of Lee for children has induced us to issue this companion book, and we feel assured no lover of the purest and highest in manhood will fail to secure a copy. The type is large and clear, and especially suited to the very young or the very old.

B. F Johnson Publishing Co., Richmond, Va.

Johnson's Readers . . .

JOHNSON'S PRIMER is the first book of this series. It is a beautiful little book, abounding in colored illustrations, containing a variety of devices, which, besides securing the learner's interest, furnish ample exercise for those of his faculties which most need early training.

"Memory Gems," little nuggets of wisdom, which are to be learned by heart, and frequently recited, are to be found on nearly every page. They are maxims of sound morality and practical knowledge. **Simple Writing Lessons** in different slants, intended as an exercise for the muscles of the little hands in making the straight and curved lines that constitute script letters, are to be found on almost every page. **Easy Drawing Lessons** are added in sufficient numbers to furnish the child ample exercise for that strong inclination—the habit of scribbling—with which nature has wisely provided child-life as an escape-valve for pent-up energy. This **Primer** was designed as the first of a series of six books. It is printed in large type upon good paper; well bound; and its pictures have been especially drawn to illustrate the thoroughly-graded and well-selected lessons.

JOHNSON'S READERS.—Johnson's First, Second, Third, Fourth, and Fifth Readers complete the series of six books. In entering upon a series of school readers, the publishers desire to call attention to some of the features which distinguish these books from other school readers, and they believe that these features will commend the books to all progressive educators.

Specially Prepared.—These books have been prepared with special reference to the practical work of the school room. The pages are not encumbered with useless matter. Whatever would be likely to divert the attention of the child from the chief object in view—that of learning to read—has been omitted or relegated to its proper place.

Thoroughly Graded and Complete.—These books contain a larger amount of reading matter than the corresponding numbers of most readers in general use; in the variety and interest of their lessons they are unsurpassed; their gradation is perfect; they form a complete, unbroken series, and are uniform as regards both matter and method.

The Best Style of Literature.—The reading lessons have been prepared with a view to cultivating a taste for the best style of literature as regards both soundness of thought and excellence of expression. While selecting the reading lessons with a view, also, to securing the learner's interest and exciting his imagination to

B. F. Johnson Publishing Co., Richmond, Va.

SOUTHERN LITERATURE By Miss LOUISE MANLY, of South Carolina. Over 500 pages; more than 50 full-page illustrations. Large 12mo.; cloth. Price, $1.00.

"SOUTHERN LITERATURE," by Miss Louise Manly, of South Carolina, is a comprehensive review, with copious extracts and criticisms, of the leading Southern productions in the literary world from 1579 to 1895. It contains an appendix with a full list of Southern authors; has over 500 pages, 12mo.; is illustrated with more than 50 full-page engravings, and substantially bound in cloth; is already used extensively in the schools of the South; and has made a favorable impression in the North and in the West.

This is one of the books referred to in Mr. Minter's able address before the Texas State Teachers' Association. The need for just such a work has been long felt, in both educational and literary circles. It is lamentable, but nevertheless true, that many of the best and brightest Southern writers are scarcely known outside the circle of their intimate friends. Their productions have either gone begging for a publisher, or been published by houses that felt very little interest in the author, and far less interest in his productions. But, fortunately, an avenue is now opening up for the dissemination of Southern literature; and all that is required for the permanent establishment of this much needed avenue is the *substantial* encouragement of Southern teachers, school officials, and patriotic citizens of all trades and professions.

SOUTHERN STATES OF THE AMERICAN UNION. By Dr. J. L. M. CURRY, of Virginia. 272 pages; large 12mo. Student's edition, plain cloth, $1.00; Library edition, $1.25.

THIS book is not controversial. Its aim is to reconstruct ideas and opinions adverse to the South, in so far as they are founded on ignorance and prejudice. It embodies in one neat and compact volume the result of the studies on Constitutional History of one of the ablest and most accomplished writers of this country. The writing of this book is timely. Some of the greatest political events of the past are being adjusted into truthful history, and new light is being added by the facile pen of a man whose master mind analyzes with the clearness and power of a spectrum. This book should have a place in the curriculum of every high-school, academy, college, and university of this country. The schools of the South can ill afford to be without it. Every citizen should have a copy in his library.

WILLIAMSON'S LIFE OF GENERAL ROBERT E. LEE. By Mrs. M. L. WILLIAMSON, of New Market, Va. Nearly 200 pages, beautifully and profusely illustrated. 12mo. Illuminated covers. Price, 25 cents. Library edition, cloth, gold stamping, 75 cents.

THE only history of that grand, good man written specially for the young. The style in which the book is written secures one's interest from the start and never lets it lag. The profuse illustrations delight older people. The book was intended originally as a gift book, but is now adapted to schools as well. The low price at which we offer it places it within the reach of all.

WILLIAMSON'S LIFE OF GENERAL "STONEWALL" JACKSON. By Mrs. M. L. WILLIAMSON, of New Market, Va. Nearly 200 pages, beautifully and profusely illustrated. 12mo. Illuminated covers. Price, 25 cents. Library edition, cloth, gold stamping, 75 cents.

THE very flattering reception given Mrs. Williamson's Life of Lee for children has induced us to issue this companion book, and we feel assured no lover of the purest and highest in manhood will fail to secure a copy. The type is large and clear, and especially suited to the very young or the very old.

www.ingramcontent.com/pod-product-compliance
Lightning Source LLC
Chambersburg PA
CBHW022137300426
44115CB00006B/227